PARABLES OF A COUNTRY PREACHER

Boyd A. Blumer

1996

SPIRITUAL GROWTH RESOURCES
A Division of Organization Resources Press
Downers Grove, Illinois

Scripture quotations from the *Revised Standard Version of the Bible*, copyright © 1946, 1952, 1971 by the Division of Christian Education, National Council of Churches are reprinted by permission.

"The Parable of the Crazy-Work Quilt" is reprinted by permission of Discipleship Resources, P.O. Box 840, Nashville, Tennessee 37202.

Permission for reprint was granted by the Wildlife Management Institute to quote from F.H. Kortright's "Ducks, Geese and Swans of North America," copyright © 1943 and from Harper and Row to quote from Eric Hoffer's "The Ordeal of Change" in A Parable of the Canadian Goose.

Published by:
Spiritual Growth Resources
A Division of Organization Resources Press
2142 Oxnard Drive
Downers Grove, Illinois 60515

First Printing 1980

Printed in the United States of America

WITH LOVE TO

My wife, EVELYN

My parents, HAROLD and OTILLIE BLUMER

My in-laws, BERNARD and EDNA ROEPKE

CONTENTS

FOREWORD

I am basically a product of the city. Most of my earlier years were spent in Seattle, the Los Angeles area, Tampa, Atlanta, Jacksonville and Indianapolis. In 1968 I was assigned to the Dakotas to become their episcopal leader. I will never forget the leaden feeling I had in the pit of my stomach as I turned my 1967 Cougar (it is now—twelve years later—a beloved member of our family) off an interstate highway and headed north on U.S. 281 across the flat plains of South Dakota. There were wheat and grass as far as the naked eye could see. There were few trees, few houses, few cars, few towns–and the towns there were seemed old and dirty. The hot summer wind was blowing. My soul felt as barren as the country-side appeared to be.

All that has changed. I love this land with its clean air, big sky and wide open spaces. I love its people with their rugged independence; their toughness in adversity; their ability to cope with the elements and overcome; their capacity for wholesome living and genuine caring. Boyd Blumer is a product of this land. He is one of its people.

The sermons in this volume do not represent the sophistication and polish of a Sockman, Sheen, Ogilvie or Schuller. These sermons, as carefully crafted as any, are down-to-earth; a sheer delight to read. They are searching, pointed, faithful and above all, imaginative. "High steeple preachers" might find the going rough out here. There is an earthy, chuckling honesty devoid of most pretension. Boyd Blumer has captured that mood–the mood of rural and small town America where half of America's Protestants still live.

The sermons are, as the title of the book suggests, parables. They reflect our Lord's approach to teaching and preaching. They take a central idea–a story–and use it for all it's worth. If you don't know about the Canadian goose, patchwork quilts, Garrison Dam, or how it feels to come in last in a two-mile race, you don't know what you're missing. Just as Jesus talked about seeds, wineskins and lost treasures, Boyd talks about butterflies, gardens and Poverty Flats. And don't miss his correspondence with Brezhnev. You'll use it–one way or another. Blumer strays from the Dakotas a time or two, to Massachusetts or New Mexico, but that can be forgiven. The flavor of the message always has the same special sort of tang. And, far more important, it is authentic.

One other thing you ought to know. I love Boyd Blumer. He has woven a butterfly rug for my wife. He made waffles and sausage for our Leslye when she was a little girl, and years later sent her a rustic, antique waffle iron when she was married. He has been a trusted, beloved pastor to our youngsters when they have moved through some private hells and climbed some wondrous mountains. He is a dear friend–cheerful, rumpled, exactly who he is. He tells a good story and he lives the story he tells. That is known as incarnational theology.

I will soon return to the city, but I will never be the same because Boyd and others like him have made me understand the sacredness of simple things, the truth to be found in unexpected places and the hardy fun to be had in embracing the basics of life close to God's good earth. You will find all of this in *Parables of a Country Preacher*.

James Armstrong
Bishop, Dakotas Area
23 February 1980

PREFACE

Two significant events converged on my life this year. One is the 100th anniversary of my home church. It stands in the open country in the heart of the Red River Valley in North Dakota. The persons in that church, like my grandfather who helped found and build it, and my dear parents are parables of life through whom God has spoken.

This year is the silver anniversary of my ordination. I have served United Methodist Churches at Goodrich and Chaseley, North Dakota; Faith Church in Aberdeen, South Dakota; Clear Lake, South Dakota and First Church, Sioux Falls, South Dakota. This book of sermons is an attempt to say "thank you" for the privilege to share in their life and faith as a minister of the Gospel.

The sermons were never prepared to be published. The parable-type sermon developed out of a study of the parables of Jesus and a continuing attempt to communicate the Gospel effectively to the people of God.

Parables are an effective way to communicate the nature, purpose and will of God. Jesus would use the ordinary events and objects, and the every day experiences of life as parables to communicate the message. The people not only recalled the parable, but also the point it made.

Parables have an appeal to a wide range of persons from the young to the old. A sermon was used for the second time in the same parish. It had been re-written but the basic story remained. An eleven year old boy reminded his parents, 'We got warmed over potatoes today." He was only six years old when the sermon was given the first time.

Parables identify with life and give it a new dimension. The hearers will have a similiar experience. They begin to reflect on how God is seeking to speak through them, or what God is calling them to be or to do, out of their own life experiences.

Parables allow the Holy Spirit to speak new truths to the listener. A parable is given. An interpretation of its meaning is presented. Often the parable prompts new thoughts and ideas and concerns, which gives it a wider interpretation.

Preaching is a continual learning experience. My best preaching teachers were my first congregations. Two-thirds of my ministry has been with "country churches." They were discriminating and perceptive. They know a good sermon and a poor one, and they will usually tell you. Often it is assumed if a church is small or rural, their faith and understandings will be simplistic. Of if a congregation is large and urban, it will be sophisticated. No such generalization can be made of either one. I have deeply appreciated the honesty and the candor, the depth of biblical and theological understandings of the congregations I have served.

I am deeply indebted to many persons and places for the germ ideas of the parables. Some are from sermons I have heard or read, or from news articles and books.

Several persons must be mentioned, for without them this book would not be published: Bishop James and Phyliss Armstrong, Rueben and Beverly Job, and Norman Shawchuck; my wife Evelyn, who not only typed the manuscript, but who has so patiently and lovingly given support and encouragement, and who has heard some of these sermons so often she could preach them herself; to our family, Craig and Bruce, who gave debators' critiques of many of these sermons. I loved that and miss it now. And to Kurt and Sue, for being patient listeners of their preacher dad. You are meaningful persons in my life, and I thank God for each of you.

Boyd A. Blumer
Sioux Falls, South Dakota
March 1980

I.
A PARABLE OF THE CANADIAN GOOSE

Consider the birds of the air . . . Matthew 6:26—

Every spring and fall when my eyes catch those long beautiful "V" shaped flights of the Canadian goose, and that sweet music of their honking fills my ears, my mind begins to whirl, my heart picks up three extra beats, and my trigger finger begins to itch — maybe this is the year I will shoot my first goose. This hope and dream has been with me for over forty years.

I will remember coming home from school with my eight year old brother and seeing geese by the hundreds cruising in just over the tree tops of our farmstead and landing in a nearby field. Our parents were not at home so we decided to get ourselves a goose. All we had was an old 12 gauge Remington pump shotgun. We weren't big enough to reach the trigger and we were fearful if we put it to our shoulder, it would knock us down. But we wanted to shoot a goose. We crawled through the cornfield and the mud until we got to a place where we could see the geese. One of us held the gun against a fence post and the other pulled the trigger. Years later we found out that the number 7-½ shot pellets we were using were fine for pheasants but not nearly heavy enough for geese.

For forty years I have wanted to shoot a goose, but now I WILL NEVER SHOOT A GOOSE. Do you know what changed my mind? I was studying the sixth chapter of Matthew where Jesus was saying,

> Look at the birds of the air, they neither sow nor reap nor gather into barns, yet your heavenly father feeds them. Are you not of much more value than they?   Matthew 6:26

Then later I read this—

> The sagacity, wariness, strength and fidelity are characteristics of the Canadian goose, which are possessed by no other bird, in the same degree. The Canadian goose in many respects may serve as a model for human beings.   From "The Ducks, Geese, Swans" of N.A. by F.H. Kortright, p. 84.

That started me on a search to know more about Canadian geese and that search changed my mind and my life. I want to share some of the fruit of that search with you in the Parable of the Goose.

1. *The need to cooperate.* Those who have studied the flight of geese have discovered geese flying in that "V" pattern, with their wings beating in rhythm, will fly 70 percent further than in the scattered pattern of ducks. The lead goose cuts a swath through the air and it provides lift for the next two birds behind it. As the lead goose begins to tire, another one moves to the front and the rest fan out along the edges for a breather. The rested ones then move to the front to take the lead.

If the national and international problem of energy, or the problems of our state and community are to be solved, we must learn from the goose. If we are to meet the opportunities for witness and ministry for Christ and the church, we must learn from the goose—learn how to cooperate, how to share in the leadership of our world, our state, our church.

This is what Jesus means when he says, "Take my yoke upon you and learn from me . . . For my yoke is easy and my burden is light." (Matthew 11:29 & 30) Our life and ministry in Christ's name is a shared ministry—with HIM—with others. It is a cooperative ministry where we are yoked together.

Was not this the kind of cooperation and working together Paul is appealing for:

> We are to grow up in every way into Him who is the head, into Christ from whom the whole body, joined and knit together by every joint with which it is supplied when each part is working properly, makes bodily growth and upbuilds itself in love.
> Ephesians 4:15 & 16.

Yes, consider the birds of the air and learn to cooperate.

2. *The need to care.* If a goose is wounded or becomes too ill or weak to continue in flight and is forced to drop out, it is never abandoned, never left alone. A pair of stronger geese will go with the weaker one to find a resting place and stay with it until it is strong enough to resume flight.

In life today, there is such a lack of caring and such a great need to care. Let me try to illustrate this in two ways:

Our congregation has now sponsored its fourth refugee family. I find an increasing number of people who are in opposition, either directly or indirectly

17

to their presence among us. How easily we forget that our nation is a nation of refugees. Both my grandfathers came to America to escape conscription into the Army. The Pilgrims and the Puritans were refugees. There are very few families in our nation who cannot find in their family tree, persons who came to this land because they were political or religious refugees. Persons who came to this land because of the horrors of war, oppression, famine and strife.

Eric Hoffer is one of my favorite contemporary writers. Listen to his insightful analysis:

> Most Americans today bristle with indignation when they are told that this country was built, largely by hordes of undesireables. This should be a cause for rejoicing. Only here in America were the common folk of the world given a chance to show what they could do on their own, without a master pushing or ordering them about.

> When lifted by the nape of the neck, these lowly peasants, shopkeepers, laborers, paupers, jailbirds and drunks, were dumped in this land and told "Go to it, it is yours."

> And they were not awed by the magnitude of the task, but hungry for action, pent up for centuries, found an outlet. They went to it with an ax, pick, shovel, plow, on foot, on horse, in wagons and on flatboats. They went to it praying, howling, singing, brawling, drinking and fighting, make way for the people!

Our caring is really "making way for people." That is what has made our land what it is and only our caring will make our land what it should be. I have studied churches trying to discover what it is that makes a church great. There are great churches with few members and with many members, but the one outstanding characteristic is how they care for people.

A few weeks ago we discovered a man wandering around the church. If he was here and you didn't see him, you could have smelled him. Alfred, to many of us, is a no-good bum. He had been sleeping for weeks in the 10th Street Bridge Hotel. The food service was not the best, mostly a liquid diet of distilled corn and grapes. The shower facilities are limited, depending on whether it is raining or not. He came to us wanting work. He would not accept our offers for food and housing without working for it. We had a few odd jobs, which he did extremely well. Off and on I engaged him in conversation, and this is his story. Alfred came from Latvia. When he was fourteen years old the Russians swept into his village and took twenty-seven persons including his mother, father, a brother, sister and some aunts and uncles and machine gunned them down. He was the only one to escape. He lived for weeks in the woods eluding capture. He served in the Underground and the United States Army for six years. He speaks and writes seven different languages.

Alfred came to America and married a girl from his homeland. They had four children, two girls who are now nurses and two sons who are making a career in the Army. His wife was killed in a car accident in St. Paul and he raised his family of four mostly by himself. With his family grown and on their own, he turned to alcohol, as he told me "TO EASE THE PAIN IN MY HEART."

Do you know any Alfreds? They are all around us, bruised and broken by the tragedy of their lives. Maybe you feel like Alfred now and then and seek for someone to ease the pain in your heart.

How great is the need to care! We cannot do everything for everybody, but if we care, we can begin today to do something for someone.

> As you did it to one of the least of these my
> brethren, you did it to me.   Matthew 25:40

Yes, consider the birds of the air and the need to care.

3. *A need to commitment.*   Geese mate for life. If either partner is killed or dies, the other never pairs up again. Both parents assume full responsibility for the young. From the time they are hatched, whether they are beginning to swim, searching for food or learning to fly - they are never without both parents.

Commitment is necessary if we are to fulfill our hopes for life. Marriage cannot be meaningful and fulfilling without a commitment to it. The family will fail without commitment.

The basic and fundamental need of your life and mine is a total commitment to Jesus Christ and His church. The basic and fundamental need of this church is a total commitment to Jesus Christ. Not expecting someone else to carry our responsibility, not running away when things are not going my way, but a commitment to Jesus Christ and His church. A commitment to pray together, to work together, to stay together, to worship together, to love and to serve together. A commitment that demands all of life.

Can you see now why, after seeking for forty years to shoot a goose, I'll never again even shoot at a goose? For as I have considered the birds of the air, as Jesus suggested, they have too much to teach us about cooperation, about caring and about commitment.

II.
A PARABLE OF THE RACE FOR LIFE

When I enrolled in college, I had visions and ambitions of earning my letter in athletics. Being something of a small high school sports hero, I soon discovered college was vastly different. I was not big enough for football, I was not tall enough for basketball and I did not have an arm for baseball. My only hope was track, but here too, I was limited. I was too small for the field events of the shot and discus. I was too slow for the dash events of the 100 and 200 yards. My only hope was the distance events.

I was not a great runner - I never would have been - but I did enjoy and still enjoy running.

My first track meet was the invitational relays at the University of South Dakota. I entered the two mile event. There were about twenty of us entered and at the crack of the gun we were off for eight long, grueling laps around the quarter mile oval track. At the end of the first lap, I was doing very well. I was leading. But with each succeeding lap, I began to lag and the more experienced and the better trained runners passed me by, one by one.

Just as I was beginning my eighth and final lap, a huge cheer went up behind me. Tom Two Hawk of the university put on a tremendous last lap spurt, running with the grace and the speed of an antelope, setting a new meet record by more than thirty-one seconds.

Can you imagine how I felt? The race was over. There was no prize to win. But then the thought occurred to me, "why not try to finish the race?" I plodded along the back stretch, barely able to pick up one foot and put the other down. As I was entering the final turn, I looked ahead and saw the workmen setting up the three foot, six inch high hurdles for the next event. I was no two-miler, much less a high hurdler; how could I ever finish the race now? Someone saw me and called out, "Clear the track, some fool is still running." The ovation I received for finishing the race was greater than the cheers given to the university runner for setting a new meet record.

Most sports are team ventures. A couple of hot shots on a basketball team can make up for less gifted players. A few good linemen can make a mediocre backfield look good. But life is more like the sport of track. I came in last, not because of anyone else, but because of me. Just me - I was not fast enough. I could have blamed someone for crowding me on the corners, I could have accused the starter for placing me on the outside lane of the third row. In life, we can fault others where we begin, or what we do not have, or what we did not receive, but in reality, the heart of the problem lies with ourselves.

The writer of the Book of Hebrews can give guidance to the Parable of the Race for Life:

23

Therefore, since we are surrounded by so great a cloud of witnesses, let us also lay aside every weight and sin which clings so closely, and let us run with perseverence the race that is set before us, looking to Jesus the pioneer and perfector of our faith, who for the joy that was set before him endured the cross, despising the shame, and is seated at the right hand of the throne of God. Hebrews 12:1 & 2

1. *People.* The writer is suggesting at the very outset that which we so easily overlook and forget. We are surrounded by a host of people, spectators, witnesses. There are many who are watching us run our race for life—our families, our children, our neighbors, our partners, our critics, and our enemies. They are all there. They cannot run our race for us; they are there to cheer us or to jeer us; they are there to encourage and to observe; they are there but we must do the running.

There are others in the grandstands of life that we fail to recognize. They are the ones who have fought and died for us to run the race. If we ever think we are solely on our own or that no one cares what we do or say, let us remind ourselves again and again that we are surrounded by a "great cloud of witnesses." Surrounded by people who do care and who are concerned that we run our race for life and that we run it well.

2. *Preparation.* In our race for life, we need to prepare. "Let us lay aside every weight and sin which clings so closely." Serious training began in

January, months before the first track meet. The basketball team was still in session, snow was knee-deep outside and we began our daily workouts of calisthenics and then running until exhausted, innumerable laps around the gymnasium floor.

As soon as the snow was off the roads, we ran outside, up and down an old hilly gravel road in the mud and slush. It was only a few weeks before the first meet that we were given our spiked shoes, and we continued our training with wind sprints, timed heats, endurance runs on the cinder based quarter mile track. Training and conditioning was an absolute necessity. The legs were strengthened. The lungs developed breath control. The heart was enabled to meet the demands for oxygen filled blood. Weeks and months were spent in preparation for a race that lasted but a few minutes. It would appear that a disproportionate amount of time was spent in preparation, but was it?

How many ideas and concerns have been inspired by God but failed because of the unwillingness of persons to prepare, to take the time to do the necessary work of study, devotion and prayer? We ministers are not exempt at this point. After a few years in the ministry, several parishes are served and a "barrel" of sermons is developed. It is always much easier to take out an old one and give it instead of going through the demanding task of study, prayer, outlining and writing.

Jesus spent years in preparation for just three years in the ministry. His effectiveness can be traced to his solid preparations. Paul spent three years in preparation

25

after his Damascus experience before he began preaching throughout the Mediterranean world. The disciples spent forty days in prayer before Peter and John began preaching with 3000 converted in a single sermon.

We must prepare to run our race for life. Either we take the time to prepare or failure and frustration will be ours.

3. *Perseverance.* We need to persevere, we need to keep going. "Let us run with perseverance the race that is set before us." The most difficult part of the race is the middle mile. Laps one and two were easy. I know, I was leading. The final laps were easier—the finish line is in view. It is the middle mile that really tests us.

Many persons make a good start in life, they get off on the right foot. They have it all going their way, but then something goes wrong. Their life begins to fall apart. Difficulties and problems arise with their family, with their business, with themselves. That's the middle mile of life.

It is during this middle mile, when one's legs become weak and begin to ache. The lungs are burning, unable to get enough air. The heart is pounding like a trip-hammer trying to keep up with the body demands for oxygen filled blood. The mouth is parched, it feels as if two large napkins are in your mouth, absorbing every drop of moisture.

The physical punishment is severe but the mental harassment is even worse. Here I was the last person in the race, eating the dust of the others and I began to think, "What are you doing out here?" "What is this going to get you?" "Why don't you quit and try

26

something easier?" "Why not do something you can be a success at, like playing tiddly-winks in the girls' dorm?"

Most of life is running during the "middle mile." It is repetitious, it is monotonous, it is burdensome. Futility, frustration and failure are the real competitors in the race for life. We begin to look for something easier—more pay and less work, more vacation and less responsibility. Some begin to look for a church that preaches "my" kind of gospel, a gospel of sweetness and ease "you are a good person," a gospel of tranquility, "you won't have to do much here," a gospel of security, "we will give you just what you want."

Every lap in the race must be run in turn. There is no such thing as running laps one and two, then sitting out the middle mile, only to re-enter again for a glorious finish of laps seven and eight. Every lap is to be run and the victory comes in running each lap well.

The most disheartening thing is to run through that middle mile, looking forward to finishing the race and then coming around that final turn, to face those three foot, six inch high hurdles.

More people have failed to finish their race for life because as they looked ahead, they saw the hurdles, hurdles they knew they could never cross so they gave up and quit. Read the biographies of some of the great lives and what made them famous. They not only had the ability to keep going during the middle mile, but when confronted with insurmountable hurdles, hurdles they knew they could not cross alone, they drew on all of their inner resources and kept on going and the hurdles faded away.

The need to run with perseverence the race that is set before us, despite discouragement and seeming defeat is a demand we all face.

4. *Power.* There is power available for the race for life. "Looking to Jesus the pioneer and perfector of our faith."

Every good runner develops what is called the "second wind." There comes a moment while running that a person is at the point of exhaustion, but then the body adapts and almost miraculously, the "second wind" comes and there is a new energy, strength and power to run.

In life, we have strength and ability to do things on our own, but if the race of life is to be finished well, a "second wind" is needed, an outside source of power. That power is available to us in Jesus Christ.

I have appreciated the way the New English Bible translates that part of our text: "With our eyes fixed on Jesus, on whom faith depends from start to finish." (12:2) That's our source of power, and the purpose for which we run. Our race for life will never be finished unless we have the power and the purpose to run that is found in Christ Jesus.

He is the one who ran the race, and ran it victoriously. He is the one who will give us the power and purpose to run our race.

The writer of Hebrews mentions an odd thing in regard to Jesus Christ, "Jesus, who for the joy that was set before Him, endured the cross." What joy is there in suffering upon a cross? Can we even partially understand the pain, the suffering, the torture of a cross, yet he says, "for the joy . . . he endured the cross."

The joy of Jesus Christ is found in that He knew whatever may happen to Him, His life was given to the will and purposes of God. Life's most satisfying joy is to know God is using my life. There is no greater joy than to know that our lives are given to God for whatever He wants, no matter what the hardship, sorrow or cross that we are called to bear.

Ordinarily the cross was a symbol of death. Has there ever been a greater tragedy on this earth than Jesus Christ, an innocent person; Jesus Christ, the Son of God, Jesus Christ, the Savior of the world condemned, convicted, crucified?

But God was there in that Life, and that Life had chosen to be obedient to God, and now for us, the cross is a symbol of joy and hope. If God was able to do that with Jesus Christ, what does God stand ready to do with your life and mine, in any circumstance we face, if we have chosen to do His will. This is our hope, that God can take our lives and use them when committed to His will and purpose.

Every four years the nations of the world gather for the Olympics. Only one person gets to wear the gold medallion in each race. There is only one winner.

But in the race of life, there are no winners and losers, there are only finishers and quitters.

> Since we are surrounded by so great a cloud of witnesses, let us lay aside every sin which clings so closely, and let us run with perseverence the race that is set before us, looking to Jesus, the pioneer and the perfector of our faith, who for the joy that was set before Him endured the cross, and despising the shame, and is seated at the right hand of the throne of God.   Hebrews 12:1-2

III.
A PARABLE OF THE
CRAZY-WORK QUILT

There is an art among our ladies that is fast falling
away, the art of making crazy-work quilts. With the
coming of thermostatically controlled electric
blankets, dacron-filled comforters, and thermo-
weave bed spreads, the art of making and stitching a
quilt is becoming a lost art.

In a former parish, we had a group of older ladies
who spent most of the winter making quilts. But they
did not make quilts the way I remember my grandmother making them.

The quilts made by these ladies were works of art—
absolutely beautiful! I called on those ladies three
times within two weeks and I had coffee with them
each time. I hinted every time that the quilt they were
making would make an excellent Christmas gift for
their pastor. (They never caught the hint.) The pattern
they were stitching was called, "The Wedding Band."
It was a series of interlocking circles, with each circle in
a different shade of brown or yellow or gold.

My grandmother would have dropped dead on
the spot had she seen those ladies buying yards of
beautiful cloth, cutting it into bits and pieces, and
then sewing them back together into the various
patterns and designs.

When my grandmother bought a whole piece of

cloth, she would make a dress, shirt or a pair of pants and save the scraps. The bits and pieces that were left over, the tail of a worn-out shirt, the pockets of an overall that could no longer be patched, the hand-me-down dress that no longer had someone to hand it to, the rags and tags, the odds and ends, the bits and pieces—this is what my grandmother would take to make into a quilt. She used these scraps and bits and pieces to make a pattern or a design of her own.

Often it was difficult to see the pattern. You had to use your imagination. But turning these left-overs into something useful became known as the stitching of a crazy-work quilt.

Often, ministers give the impression that they are always happy and everything is moving along beautifully. I recall early in my ministry, I came to church early to pray and meditate, to prepare my own heart and soul for the services of the day. I had worked hard on the sermon, but it just did not seem to fit. The scripture text was from Isaiah, and he was speaking confidently, "Thus saith the Lord." There was not a word like that on my lips.

What should I say? What could I say? It was now too late to find a new text and begin over. I had no "barrel" of sermons to draw upon.

I looked across those empty pews and began to picture in my mind the persons I could expect to be there.

There would be Les and his family. His wife had died leaving two small children. He was spending over seventy-five dollars a month just for medicine for his anemic and diabetic ten year old daughter. I knew every dollar he gave to the church was food off

31

his table and clothes off his back.

Marie would be there in her usual place—the fourth pew from the front on the right side—always saving enough room at the end of the pew for her husband who had passed away five years ago.

Old granddad—a saint if I ever met one—who could not hear a single word I said because of deafness. He would look up at me with his beaming face, and again and again I said to myself, "Granddad, you are preaching to me."

Maybe Otto and his wife would be there. Their daughter was in the process of getting a divorce. The two grandchildren were living with them. The agony of their hearts could be seen in the lines on their faces. But what could I do about it?

Malcolm and his family never missed. He told me once he could not remember the last time he had sinned, but he could name the sins of everyone else, especially mine. He had a third grade education, but he had a photographic memory. I am convinced he could begin with Genesis 1:1 and not miss over a thousand verses of 23,214 verses in the entire Bible. He was a tough one for a young preacher to face.

But God never leaves us standing alone. Arnold and Helen would be there to put their arms of love and prayer and support around their pastor and their church.

And as I looked at that congregation I thought—if ever there was a crazy-work quilt, that was it. What could I say? What could I do? Who would listen? Was there a pattern or design? Who could see it? But now I know that congregation was not unusual.

Have you ever secretly wished you could be in a church where Jesus Christ was the minister, and the disciples would be the official board? I doubt if I would ever want to be in such a church.

Let's start out with Peter. Do you recall how angry Peter could become? Do you remember how he could cuss and swear? He didn't care what he said or who heard it.

James and John—another pair of hot-heads. If you were their friends, that was great, but if you crossed them, they would call fire from heaven upon you. They would just as soon see you dead as alive.

There was Nathaniel. He went along for the good time. He thought it was a good deal. He had heard and seen enough of this Jesus to know that this was a good thing. He wanted in on it. If it flopped, that was all right with him—nothing ventured, nothing gained.

Matthew was a tax-collector—a political job. A job you got by rubbing the backs of the right people. The last person one would ever want on your official board would be Mattahew but there he was!

How about Simon? Simon, a Zealot, had signed an oath in his own blood to overthrow Rome. He was an insurrectionist. He was part of a dedicated underground. The only decent respectable person in the whole group was Judas. He was the kind of person you would respect. The other eleven thought so highly of Judas they gave him the honor and responsibility of keeping their money. They didn't trust each other, but Judas they trusted.

Even if Jesus Christ would be the minister of that

church, would you continue to come and give and participate with such persons on the board?

Was there a pattern or a design? Who could see it?

Take a look at any congregation. It is more like a crazy-work quilt than a whole piece of cloth made into a useful garment. We are not alike in our looks or our dress. We are not alike in our families or our wealth. We are not alike in our depth or reality of spiritual experience. We are more like bits and pieces put together because we happen to be a part of this congregation. Is there a pattern or a design here? Who can see it?

Or look at our very own lives! Do you feel like a whole piece of cloth, made into some useful garment? Or do you know that there are some worn spots, there are patches, there are ripped and frayed ends? Is there a pattern or a design in your life? In mine? Who can see it?

Has it ever occurred to you that all God has to work with are the rags and tags, the odds and the ends, the bits and pieces? This is what God takes and uses to weave and to sew the quilt of life, a crazy work quilt that will have a pattern, a design. Now you and I may not see that pattern. You and I may not know the design, but it is there, and it is God's pattern and God's design—not yours, not mine, not ours but His.

Our task is to find where our bit or piece fits into the design. There will be times when we must cut and trim our piece to blend in with the other pieces in the design. This is difficult for most of us, because we like to think it is the other pieces that need to be trimmed and shaped.

Take our very lives—why should God continue to put up with our sins and our failures?

Why is God so patient and merciful to us? We are his children, but we spend so little effort knowing who our Father is. He has a will and a purpose for us, but we have neither the courage nor the faith to see what this involves. Patiently God is seeking to take the bits and pieces of our lives and use them, to bless all mankind and to hasten the coming of His kingdom.

God has a plan; God has a purpose; God has a pattern for every one of those bits and pieces, those rags and tags, those odds and ends of our lives, of the church, of the whole kingdom of God.

God is at work among us right now, seeking to fit those pieces together into the quilt of life.

We can either seek to keep our piece and try to make our own quilt to our design, or we can seek to place what we have and what we are, into God's hands, and let Him use it as he seeks to complete the beautiful design of His creation.

IV.
A PARABLE OF THE GARRISON DAM

You are the Light of the world. A city set on
a hill cannot be hid. Nor do men light a lamp
and put it under a bushel, but on a stand,
and it gives light to all in the house. Let your
light so shine, that they may see your good
works and give glory to your Father in
heaven.   Matthew 5:14-16.

In Him was life, and the life was the light
of men. The light shines in the darkness and
the darkness had not overcome it. The true
light that enlightens every man was coming
into the world.   John 1:4,5,9

I am the light of the world; He who
follows me will not walk in darkness, but
will have the light of life.   John 8:12

The word "light" is a most descriptive word for
Jesus Christ. The Gospel of John uses it twenty-three
times.

The Greek have several descriptive words for light,
one of which is "phos," meaning "the light without
which life is impossible." "Phos" is the word used in
each of our texts for the day.

As we proceed, keep in mind our text from John:
"I am the light of the world," and our text from
Matthew: "You are the light of the world" and the
Greek description of this word light: "the light with-
out which life is impossible."

The Garrison Dam in North Dakota is one of the great marvels of construction in our day. It is one of the largest earth filled dams in the world. Hundreds of thousands of cubic yards of dirt was moved to form it. A hugh lake was created that stretches several hundred miles with over a thousand miles of shore line. It is a vital source of water for a huge irrigation system. It has gigantic electrical generators, providing electricity for much of the upper midwest region. While touring this structure the Colonel in charge made several significant statements that I wish to use to guide our thoughts today.

1. *"We do not make power here, we just transform it"* was his first statement.

There is no better description of the purpose of the church or of our own witness to Jesus Christ than that "We do not make power here; we transform it." We do not create the power, the light, the life we have in Jesus Christ. It is given by God through His Holy Spirit. We are here to transform that power into reality, into deed, into life. The light of God is what we are to transform by giving our witness of who we are, what we do, and what we stand for. Jesus Christ is the Light of the World, the light without which life is impossible. We do not invent it. It is a gift to be received, and to be transformed into life and being through our lives.

Jesus Christ demonstrated most effectively the transforming power of God in one person's life. God is present here in our world with light and power. God is present here in our lives with light and power. We do not make that power. We are to transform it

37

so that others may see our good works and give glory to God. So that the light will shine in the darkness of our world and no one shall have to walk in the darkness of life but they will have the light of life.

2. *"There is no real difference between the old fashioned water wheel and the modern day turbines, except for one thing: 'the co-efficient of friction'"* was the Colonel's second statement.

The old water wheel is often seen in pictures but it is seldom used today. The water wheel was a very inefficient way to transform power. It used too much water to grind the wheat or to saw the wood.

The Colonel went into great detail describing the electrical turbines. These turbines are highly efficient because of the pitch of the propeller blades and the design of the shafts and bearings. It was not that the old mill wheel did not work, but it took the modern day miracles of design and development to manufacture turbines that would reduce the friction, to increase the production, which is the co-efficient of friction.

Think of yourself and of the church as instruments of God to transform power. How efficient are they? What is our co-efficient of friction? What is the relationship between our potential and our production?

Must we not confess our sins to God and to each other? We have resisted being those who transform the power of God into life. It is our sin of friction with each other that is wasting our potential. It is our sins that keep us from transforming the power of God into productivity by not praying and working and sharing with each other.

We have been more concerned with "my wishes" and "my will" than we have with God's wishes and God's will. The Church of Jesus Christ by its very nature is not a one person show. It is sharing, working, praying with and for each other. This is not easy—it is difficult. This is where the friction comes in. Each of us is a person who sees and responds to life and God differently. God demands that we transform His power to decrease the friction and increase the production.

Let me go at this same concern from another direction. In our first parish we lived only sixty miles from the Garrison Dam. On a beautiful spring day, our electricity was suddenly cut off for twenty minutes. We did not think too much about it until we read in the paper the next day that over one-half of the state had been without electricity for those twenty minutes. A caretaker at the dam carelessly threw a broom that hit a switch that broke a circuit that left 300,000 people without light or power for twenty minutes.

Reflect again on your own life for a moment. How carelessly we swing our brooms that break the circuits of God's power. "My hurt feelings," "The chip on my shoulder," "My little excuses for myself," "My great expectations of others," "The easy demands I make of myself," "The burdens I place on others." All are brooms that break the circuits and cuts us off from God's power.

We can be centers and sources of light and power. We can help to carry the light and power without which life is impossible. But think of all the things we do and say that break those circuits of God's light and power. Let us seek God's forgiving grace. Let us seek the forgiveness of others, to complete the circuits and to continue to channel the light and power.

3. *"To wheel the power from the point of generation to the point of need"* is the third statement I recall.

After we completed the inside tour of the facility, the Colonel took us to the "operations office." On the wall was a huge map of the entire upper midwest area. He pointed to Watertown, South Dakota. The electrical transmission lines in a five state area all come to a center there. With the turning of a dial, or the pulling of a switch, the power generated in one area can be channeled to any other area. It does not make any difference who generates the power, The Corps of Engineers, a private company, a municipal company, they are able at this facility in the words of the Colonel, "To wheel the power from the point of generation to the point of need."

We need to see more clearly how our church is seeking to "wheel the power of Jesus Christ from the points of generation," which is really God at work in your life and mine, "to the points of need" which is the world over.

I have shared with many of you my experience with the church in Liberia, West Africa. I have said it before and I will say it again. I have never been so grateful or so proud to be a part of the Church of Jesus Christ as I was after I saw and participated in what the church is doing in Liberia. But one of the biggest stumbling blocks to the growth and development of the church in Africa is the church in America.

Liberia is a desperately poor country. The church cannot exist without mission support. The church is growing ten times faster in Liberia than here in America. But they have a hundred times less to work with. They would be growing even faster if we could only love and trust our Christian brothers and sisters to use the money we give and which they need so desperately. We actually limit the spread of the gospel and the growth of the church because of all the strings we attach to our giving. If we are to wheel the power from the point of generation to the point of need, the demand is to love, to trust, to have faith in the rest of the family of God, without regard to whom the credit belongs.

The point is this: We have the power. We have the transmission lines through the structure of the church to wheel the power to the points of need. But to do this, we must love. We must trust. We must go the second mile. We must believe. We must have faith. The church can be a center of power, the transforming power of Jesus Christ to wheel the power and the light of Christ from the point of generation to the point of need, the light and power without which life is impossible.

Let me end where I began:

1. "I am the Light of the World. You are the Light of the World." We do not make the power here, we are to transform it into life and being.

2. "People do not light a lamp and put it under a bushel." Let us consider our co-efficiency of friction, so that the friction will be reduced and the production increased.

3. "The Light shines in the darkness and the darkness has not overcome it." We can throw our brooms around, but we will not stop the light. We will only break the circuits that will put someone else in darkness.

4. "Let your light so shine" so that we will "wheel" the power from the point of generation to the point of need.

Jesus Christ is the Light of the World. The light without which life is impossible. He is the Light we bring.

We are the Light of the World. The Light our world needs. The only Light of God many will ever see is the Light of our witness.

V.
A PARABLE OF POVERTY FLATS

How beautiful upon the mountains are the feet
of him who brings good tidings, who publishes
peace, who brings good tidings of good, who
publishes salvation, who says to Zion, Your
God reigns.   Isaiah 52:7

August 24, 1945 was the greatest day in the history
of Walcott, North Dakota. What happened that day
never happened before and nothing like it has
happened since. And it will never happen again,
because one of these days the town will be totally
dead. They will pull out the trees, bury the old
foundations and farm it. August is the heart of the
harvest season, one of the busiest times of the year,
but hundreds of people left their work and gathered
in Walcott.

The only store in town housed the central telephone office. Bertha ran the store, was the post-
master and the telephone operator. She gave several
general calls over all the telephone lines that day.
"Come to town today to the victory celebration."
And everyone came. By the time our family arrived,
people were already driving up and down the
streets—honking their horns, shouting, shooting
shotguns and firecrackers. Soon everyone gathered
around the town water pump in front of the store
and post office. The self-appointed mayor, who was

also the depot agent, climbed the railing that was around the town pump and began his speech beginning with words from our text: "We have good news of great joy—the war is over—peace has come—our boys will be home soon." He went on to praise the families who had given of their sons to serve. He asked our minister to offer a prayer. He gave a special prayer for those who had lost sons, fathers, husbands and brothers in the war.

My home church had nine boys in the Armed Services and five them were killed in action. I can still visualize the service flag that hung in our little church with its blue stars and its gold stars.

There was shouting and laughter; there were tears and hand shaking and back slapping. August 24, 1945 was the greatest day ever in Walcott, North Dakota for the good news had come, the war was over.

1. *The Messenger is the Message.* To really understand the power and the potency of this word "good news" we need to look at its original meaning. The Greek word used in our text is the word, "evan-gel-ion." It is the root word for our word of evangelism or evangelical. The biblical authors chose this word very carefully because of its meaning and understandings.

"Good News": evan-gel-ion means a messenger who is the message. The word is not a noun, but an action verb.

In the days of the Old Testament, the method used to send a message was by the means of a runner—no telegraph—no telephone—no television—no satellites.

Someone had to personally carry the message. The men of the village or the nation would gather and arm themselves and go off to war. They would be gone for weeks, often for months. Certain were chosen to stay at home to guard the village from the marauding bands that roamed the area. They were not only the local militia but they were also the watchmen, who were posted in towers that surrounded the town to watch for the runners coming with the news of the battle. In order to transmit the message as quickly as possible, the runners would climb certain designated hills or mountains, often several miles from the city and wave a palm branch to signify the victory—the war was over—peace had come, soon the troops would be home.

Keeping in mind the runner who is bringing the message and the watchmen waiting to see him come, let me read again our text from Isaiah 52:

> How beautiful upon the mountains are the feet
> of him who brings good tidings, who publishes
> peace, who brings good tidings of good, who
> publishes salvation, who says, "Your God
> reigns." Hark, your watchmen lift up their
> voice, together they sing for joy; . . . they see
> the return of the Lord.

Can you see how that word was carefully chosen? In Jesus Christ - The Victory is Won! That is the Good News the world is waiting to hear. Our sins can be forgiven. The life in Christ can be lived. There is to be peace and joy in the land. The reign and rule of God is here. God has acted. God has come to earth in

Jesus Christ our Lord. Send the Messenger — Bring the Good News: "How beautiful upon the mountains are the feet of those who bring good tidings, who publish peace, who say our God reigns!"

The Messenger is the Message. The messenger is the sign that God has acted. The messenger is God's Good News of victory, of peace, of joy.

2. *We are now the Messenger who is the Message.* One of our neighbors did not come to Walcott that day. Their son was a fighter pilot and his plane did not return. The family received a telegram stating he was "missing in action." They were happy the war was over, but they could not join the celebration.

Months passed by before a military car drove into the yard to tell the family they had found their son's wrecked plane on a hillside of an island in the North Sea. I remember the family saying, "The minute we saw the car drive into our yard we knew LeRoy was dead." The did not have to be told—the Messenger was the Message.

My good people, are you aware that WE are the messengers who are the message? The Good News of Jesus Christ is not a yesterday experience or event. The Good News is now or it is not at all. If the Messenger is the Message, and if we are now that Messenger, what is the Message we carry? When we drive into someone's yard, when we enter someone's home, what is the message we carry? Look again at the world about us, a world torn by strife and war, a community with hurt and pain, a people filled with doubt and fear, our lives have been touched by Jesus

Christ and His church. We profess a faith in Jesus Christ. What is the Message we give?

We are now the Messengers who are the message. Our message is to be one of victory in Jesus Christ. Our message is to be one of joy in life. Our message is to be one of peace in the land. Messengers who are the message of what God has done in Jesus Christ. Messengers who are the message of what God can do in Christ Jesus. Messengers who are the message of what God is doing in Christ Jesus.

The watchmen of the world are waiting for those who will stand upon the mountain, who bring good tidings, who publish peace, who say, "OUR GOD REIGNS."

3. *We have the Message.* When the victory in battle was won, more than one runner was sent. The risks and dangers were many. The first runner who returned kept the palm branch.

How do we feel about the message that is ours to carry? What have we done with the message we have been given? Do we say, "It's not important" or "They already know" or "They really don't want to know" or "Let them ask me"?

We have been content to walk leisurely along the easy road in the valley. We have been too lazy to climb the mountain to signal the word. But as messengers who become the message we have a responsibility to God and the world about us. The old spiritual has really caught the spirit of the text: "Go tell it on the mountain, over the hills and everywhere; go tell it on the mountain, that Jesus Christ is born." "O how beautiful upon the mountains are the feet of those who bring good tidings, who publishes peace, who bring good tidings of good, who publish salvation, who says, 'Your God reigns.'"

47

VI.

A PARABLE OF A REVOLUTION

"As Thou didst send me into the world, so I have sent them into the world."   John 17:18

I have had an interesting exchange of fictitious letters that I wish to share with you. It is an exchange of letters with Leonid Brezhnev. This is my first letter to him.

Dear Mr. Brezhnev:

Many of the leaders of the organization I am associated with have been calling for change. They keep on telling us all the things we ought to be doing to change the world. But not too much seems to be happening. Since you are nearing retirement, you may have had opportunity to reflect on the leadership you have given your nation. It has created so much change in our world, and problems for my own nation, I might add. It occurred to me that we may have something to learn from you. Would you answer my letter and give me a few pointers? I am sure it would be most interesting to our organization.

Sincerely yours, Boyd Blumer

Here is his answer.

Dear Mr. Blumer:

I have received your letter with deep interest. Is South Dakota someplace in the United States? It is anything like Siberia? You are too vague about the revolution you want to pull off. Could you fill me in on your strengths and your resources? Many revolutions have floundered because they were not clear about their real potential.

Your comrade, Leonid Brezhnev

Dear Mr. Brezhnev:

I am sorry that I wrote in such great haste that I forgot to give you more details. Allow me to clear up a few items first. South Dakota is not like Siberia. In fact, we think it is the best place in the world in which to live. You ought to come and visit us sometime.

You are talking about revolution. I didn't mean something as drastic as that. But I will try to tell you something of our strength and potential. I will try to use some terms not familiar to us, but from what I know of you, they will have more meaning for you. In our local unit, we have 2,705 card carrying members of this community of 100,000. About 1,000 will show up for an hour each week for a special meeting. We have 400 children and youth who come for special activities, music and study each week. We have only 50 adults who will come an extra night each week for a special study meeting. But they are mostly our older, more faithful ones. We seem to do a better job of getting our women involved in activities than our men. Last year we raised over $350,000.00 through

49

our unit, but as you can quickly figure out that is about $125.00 for each card carrying member, which amounts to $2.50 per week. That is nowhere near our potential, for most of us will spend twice that much just going out for dinner each week. Well, this is a little longer than I expected. I was carried away for a moment. In the next few weeks, they will be setting my salary for next year; well, you know what I am getting at.

Hopefully yours, Boyd Blumer

Dear Mr. Blumer:

I am astounded by your last letter. I am absolutely amazed. It is a revolutionists' paradise. Before I give you some of our secrets, I have some more questions. Do you have a place to operate from? Are your members well distributed throughout your community? A successful revolution must have key people, well informed at all points.

As Ever, Leonid

Dear Leonid Sir:

I am happy to report positive answers to your questions in your last letter. For nearly a 100 years, we have had an ideal place for the center of our operations. We have one large hall that holds 1,000 people. There are over twenty other rooms that can be used for meetings of various sizes. We are located almost in the center of our city. We have weekly meetings three times on Sunday, with two educational sessions on Sunday, plus many other groups that meet at least monthly. We think our basic handbook is in every home, but we do not know how much it is read. We have a weekly newsletter that goes into every home. If something special comes along, we can let our people know quickly because we do not have restrictions on the mail service.

I am pleased to report our members are distributed throughout our entire city and the farms and villages that surround us. We have business people, professional people, farmers, teachers, and workers of every kind. I am also proud to report many of these persons have taken an active role in their civic responsibilities. We have persons in our governmental and public school offices. When I compare our members to our competitors, I can safely and humbly say, we have nothing but the best.

Sincerely, Boyd

Dear Boyd:

What are you waiting for? Take over the place! If you can't do it with that kind of potential and possibility, hire a few of my people, and we will show you how. By the way, what have you been doing for the last 100 years? What is your purpose for being around that long? Much disturbed with you, Lenny.

Dear Lenny:

You have raised some tough questions in your last letter. "What is our purpose?" you ask. That is a good question. I guess I haven't thought much about that.

You keep on talking about a takeover and a revolution. We really didn't have that in mind. We just wanted to make a few changes here and there, to keep our people happy and satisfied. Well, I might as well come straight out with it, we are jumping our proposed budget over $25,000.00. We want to find an easy way to get the money we need without having anyone get mad or leave us.

Kind of mixed up, Boyd

Dear Wishy Washy:

When we first started our letter writing to each other, I was deeply impressed by your openness and courage to write to me for advice and help. I was even considering inviting you to see me. I was preparing to make you an offer you could not refuse. Don't you believe in what you are doing? Don't you have a direction and a goal of what you want accomplished? It seems to me you just want to sit around and play tiddly winks and footsy in a day of revolution. You have everything and more to work with except one thing, and that is commitment. As far as I am concerned, this is my last letter to you. I do not have time or energy to waste on people who don't know where they are going, or how they are going to get there, or the commitment and dedication to make it happen. Personally, I hope your finance campaign fails. You probably do not earn the money they pay you now.

L. Brezhnev

Need I tell you that the letters I just read were imaginery, but the issues they raised are real.

The city of Chicago has a river running through it. Years ago they redesigned the river and changed the flow of the river because it would better suit the needs of Chicago. It appears to me we have done a similar thing with the faith we hold in Jesus Christ and His Church. We have changed our commitments to suit our needs and our hopes and we have forgotten what God had in mind for us in the first place.

"As Thou didst send me into the world, so I have sent them into the world." John 17:18

The revolution of the Church is to bring the spirit of Jesus Christ to bear upon this world by our actions and decisions. The revolution of the Church is to infiltrate this world with the love of God and the righteousness of God until our homes, our businesses, our government, our schools are under the mastery and power of Jesus Christ.

We have the resources. We have the ability. We have everything we need, except one thing. We lack the commitment and the dedication to do it. That commitment and dedication comes from our being convinced of the reality and the power of Jesus Christ. When we have experienced that reality we will know there can be no other way than the way of Jesus Christ through His Church.

"As Thou didst send me into the world, so I have sent them into the world." John 17:18

VII.
A PARABLE OF VINCE LOMBARDI
Isaiah 35

"Vince Lombardi, the total enemy of mediocrity" is the opening sentence of a report on the life of this legendary professional football coach. Vince Lombardi took the coaching job for a very mediocre football team, the Green Bay Packers. They won only one football game the previous year. In the nine seasons under his coaching, the team compiled a record of 89 wins, 29 losses and 4 ties. They won five league championships, six divisional championships and two super bowls. Vince Lombardi was the total enemy of mediocrity.

Isaiah tells us Israel was the perfect example of mediocrity. They were a defeated and discouraged nation. They were servants to a foreign power. The golden years of their greatness was past and all but forgotten.

Isaiah came preaching like an inexperienced, know-it-all seminary graduate. What did he know about what life is really like? Didn't he know how powerful they were? Couldn't he see how strong Assyria was? The beloved temple was in ruins. The government had collapsed. The army was in no condition to defend anything. There were a small group of stragglers with some faint hopes that they might be the people of God, but even those hopes were about to be crushed.

We will use the 35th chapter of Isaiah to guide our thoughts, using football terminology.

1. *The Pre-Season.* From six to eight weeks before the regular season begins, professional football teams gather for the pre-season practice. Three to four times as many players are invited to the football camp than will make the team. This is done for several reasons. The coaches are looking for the right players who will be in proper condition to play and who will learn the plays of the team. Most of the players hate the pre-season. It is long and hard and tedious. But finding the right players is a must; conditioning is a must, learning the plays is a must.

Listen to Isaiah's pre-season schedule: "Strengthen the weak hands, and make firm the feeble knees. . . . Say to those who are of a fearful heart, 'Be strong, fear not! Behold your God.'" Isaiah 35:4

If we do not want to come to the pre-season to strengthen our weak hands through a total commitment; if we do not want to come to the pre-season to make firm feeble knees through prayer; if we do not want to come to the pre-season to learn the plays of the great play maker through a study of His word, then don't expect to be on God's team when the game is played! Commitment, prayer, worship, church school, choir, committees are all vital parts of the pre-season to be a part of the team, to get into condition and to learn the plays.

Everyone wants to be on a winning team, but there is no Super Bowl, unless there is a long, hard, tedious pre-season.

2. *The Game Plan.*   Before every game is played, a game plan is developed. Out of all the possible plays, certain plays are selected to be used in the game. Vince Lombardi was a master of the game plan. From the scouting reports of the opposition's strengths and weaknesses, and from his assessment of his own team, he would select the plays that took them to victory again and again.

What was Isaiah's game plan?

> The eyes of the blind shall be opened, and the ears of the deaf unstopped; then shall the lame man leap like a hart, and the tongue of the dumb sing for joy. For waters shall break forth in the wilderness, and streams in the desert; the burning sand shall become a pool and the thirsty ground springs of water."
> Isaiah 35:5,6,7

One of the things that make great people great is the ability not to see things as they are but as they could be. All around Isaiah there were sick, weak, helpless people. He lived in an arid desert, but he saw a happy, healthy, free people living in a Garden of Eden.

"Ah," says the skeptic, "it's only a dream. The world is full of dreamers." This is no dream, it is the promise of God.

That's our game plan, not our dreams and visions, but the promise of God. Those who have won victories in the face of sure defeat have been those who refused to describe where they were in negative terms. The game plan of God is to see hope and promise where we are.

The book written a generation ago by Ole Rolvagg,

Giants In The Earth is a story of Norwegian immigrants settling in the Midwest. It is a study of two attitudes of life, Per Hansa and his wife. When Per Hansa saw the dry rolling plains of the upper Midwest, he saw it with all the hope, promise and possibility of an irrigated California Valley. All his wife could see was imaginary "giants in the earth" coming to devour her. Her vision of the future was blocked by the memory of the past, while she yearned and cried for the beauty and the majesty of the mountains and fjords of Norway. Per Hansa dreamed and toiled to make the Midwest plains blossom.

To have the insight of Moses is to see Holy Ground, where others see only sand and sagebrush and scraggly sheep and goats, and to know the game plan, the promises of God.

The game plan of God for our world is to have beauty restored, wounds healed, sorrow lifted, safe roads built, all people living as brothers and sisters and knowing the joy and peace of Christ. That's our game plan. The promises of God will not fail even in the amidst of war, inflation, energy shortage, nuclear scares, floods and all the rest.

The game plan of God is to change the Saharas of life into the Gardens of Eden and only those who have been through the pre-season, those who are in condition to play, and who know the play book of God, will be there when the Super Bowl is won.

3. *The Super Bowl.* The pre-season is long past. Many game plans have been devised and carried out. Now the final game is being played.

One of the never to be forgotten games in the annals

of football history took place on December 31, 1967. Green Bay was playing Dallas. Over 50,000 fans came out on a day when the temperature was twenty degrees below zero to see the game. It had been a tremendously hard-fought game. Green Bay was on the Dallas one yard line. There were six seconds left in the game. Green Bay was behind 17-14, and it was the fourth and final down.

They could kick a sure three point field goal and tie the score and go into sudden death overtime. They could try to pass over the super tough Dallas "doomsday" defensive line. If the pass failed, Dallas would win. Vince Lombardi called the play no one said he should have called. All football lovers know what happened. Bart Starr took the ball on a quarterback sneak over right guard with Jerry Kramer leading the way, scored the touchdown and won the game.

The Green Bay players hated that play. They had run it hundreds of times in practice, perfecting every blocking and running assignment. Now the months of practice paid off.

"And a highway shall there be and it shall be called the Holy Way." Isaiah 35:8 The unclean, the fools, the lions will not be there. They would have been weeded out in the pre-season. "But the redeemed shall walk there." Isaiah 35:9 The redeemed would be the players in the Super Bowl. The redeemed would be those who made that crucial six second play. "And the ransomed of the Lord shall return, and come to Zion with singing and everlasting joy upon their heads." Isaiah 35:10a They would be the 50,000 and more who had suffered through those long torturous losing seasons. Now their team had won!

The hated pre-season would be forgotten. The many game plans would be forgotten. But the Super Bowl would never be forgotten. "They shall obtain joy and gladness, and sorrow and sighing shall flee away." Isaiah 35:10b

The Church is not in the Super Bowl. But I pray, I dream, I see the promises of God. Are you going to join the team? That is the call of God today, to join the team, get in condition to play, and to know the plays of God's game.

VIII.

A PARABLE OF
GHOST RANCH
Luke 12:22

Northern New Mexico is an area of stark and beautiful contrasts. It is noted for its rugged mountains, multi-colored buttes, broad valleys of watered grasslands, orchards, and dry desert areas. Many rivers and streams begin here that eventually wind their way to the Rio Grande River and finally empty into the Gulf of Mexico.

By following the river system, the early Spanish conquistadors made their way into this area. Many people who still live there very proudly trace their heritage to the royal families of Spain. In those valleys with the abundant grass, they raised herds of cattle and sheep to export the hides and wool back to their homeland in Spain.

These mountains, valleys and streams attracted another group of people, the frontiersmen and hunters. They led the way for future settlements, by exploring and charting this new land. They came for the game that was in abundance, the deer, elk, and bear, but especially the beaver. Kit Carson, the folk hero of New Mexico, is such a person.

The fad of the day was to wear a broadtail beaver hat. Like the buffalo of the plains which was slaughtered for the tongue, the beaver of the mountains was slaughtered for the tail.

The Rio Grande Valley, with its tributary waters, attracted particular groups of people, people who were willing to take huge risks with the hope of getting rich quick. It was cattle for the Spaniards and hunting for the frontiersmen.

Today, there are not fertile, grassy valleys, unless they are irrigated. It is mostly arid land with cactus, weeds and blowing sands. There are deep ravines and gullys because of the eroding rains. One can look at the beautiful mountains, and stand in awe of the colored sandstone hills and not see the sickness of the land. One may marvel at the beauty of the cactus in bloom, with its red and yellow blossoms and not see the conditions that created this barren land.

The cattlemen brought too many sheep and cattle into the grassy valleys. They overgrazed the land and with the native grasses gone the door was open for wind and water to erode the soils. They brought weed seeds from Europe that have thrived because the native grasses are gone.

When the hunter came, he assumed there would be a never ending source of game. So he shot the beaver with reckless abandon, unaware of the consequences of destroying the world's finest water control artists. With the beaver gone, there was no one to build the dams to control the rushing waters of the streams, thus creating the gullies and washouts.

In the midst of this barren area stands Ghost Ranch, a ranch of 23,000 acres, given to the United Presbyterian Church. Ghost Ranch exists for two fundamental purposes. One is to restore the land. It may take 30, 50 or 100 years to restore the natural grasses. With the use of check-dams in the gullies and terraces on the hillsides to slow down the rushing waters, they hope to encourage the return of the beaver.

The second purpose is to restore people, people who come from Maine to California and from around the world to share in the seminars and the studies covering a wide range of interests and concerns.

Ghost Ranch is a living parable that raises three questions:

1. *What Can I Get Out of It?*   The destruction of the land was created by persons who came into this area with just one question in mind, "What can I get out of it?" The cattlemen brought in more cattle than the land could support. The hunter came taking more game than he could use.

This selfish, greedy question is so much a part of all of our lives. People look at their government asking, "What can I get out of it?" People even look at their church asking only, "What can I get out of it?"

This is one of life's most dangerous questions, for it considers neither God nor neighbor, only self. It does not care who it hurts or what the consequences may be. This question eats at the very heart of the church and at the heart of the democracy of this country in which we live.

This question "What can I get out of it?" makes deserts out of fertile valleys. It makes one's soul and life dry and arid. It only seeks to receive from, to be given to, to be provided for. It does not seek to give, to bless, or to renew.

2. *How Can I Work With God and Others?* The joy and the hope of Ghost Ranch is a question that is the direct opposite of the first. It asks, "How can I work with God and others?" How can a broken and sick land be healed? How can distressed, tired and wornout persons be renewed and revived?

Every person has hopes and dreams for themselves, for their church, for their community, and for their country. All of us want to see the ugly problems of our world solved. Each of us have visions of the power and the joy of Jesus Christ working in the lives of people. This question, "How can I work with God and others?" needs to be considered seriously.

God has a dream for His world. A dream that seeks to be accomplished in and through the lives of persons, like you and me. This is the privilege and the opportunity that God offers to us in Jesus Christ through His church.

3. *What Are You Going To Do With What You Have?* Mr. Arthur Pack was a magazine editor and a person of moderate means. Like many people he wanted to buy some land. Ghost Ranch came up for sale at a very reasonabale price, so he bought it and moved to live on the ranch.

As he lived there, he developed a deep love for the people and the land. He saw these people with a great heritage living in poverty. For five generations many of these people have been eking out a survival. Mr. Pack's father had given him a rare stamp collection. He sold the stamp collection and gave $400,000 to the United Methodist Church to add a hospital to their thriving mission work in the valley. There is now a 70 bed, well-run hospital in Espanola, New Mexico serving the people in the area.

Mr. Pack found that he could not run the ranch as it needed to be run. He wanted someone to come and restore the land to its original greatness, and to provide Christian ministry to people. The United Presbyterian Church accepted his offer and is faithfully and steadily at work bringing renewal to land and people.

What are you going to do with what you have? Keep it? Hoard it? Die with it? Or will we "Provide ourselves with purses that do not grow old, with a treasure in the heavens that does not fail . . . . For where your treasure is, there will you heart be also." Luke 12:33-34.

Few of us may ever have the opportunity or the means to do what Pack has done, but the question is still ours to answer. Into our hands and into our lives, God has given many things. It may be only the "widow's mite" in our eyes, but God does not see or count the way we do. God will ask each of us, "What are you going to do with what you have?"

Mr. Pack can drive into Espanola and see people being healed who would otherwise suffer greatly or die prematurely. He can see 3,000 people a year come to Ghost Ranch for study and prayer and renewal. He can see a land beginning to return to its former beauty and abundance. He has a treasure of joy and satisfaction that most of us and the world are searching for, because he did something with what he had.

Ghost Ranch is a living parable that confronts us all with the basic questions of life and faith.

IX.
A PARABLE OF THE
PICTURES OF LIFE
Matthew 7:1-14

The Babson Institute of Business Administration, Babson Park, Massachusetts, has erected a twenty-five ton globe in the center of the campus. This immense monument is 28 feet in diameter, with a scale of thirty miles to the inch. It is cast in twenty different colors. Every country of the world is pictured. Every mountain range and valley is in proper scale. The deserts, forests, grasslands, rivers, lakes, the major cities are all identified. It is made with removeable panels so if the boundaries of a nation change, that panel is removed, and recast to indicate those changes.

Each day as the students go to class they see the world before them. The administration was asked why they had the huge globe erected and their answer was, "We want our students more world minded and less provincial in their thinking and acting."

If an institution like the Babson Institute is deeply interested in and committed to having their students with a global outlook on life, how much greater is the demand upon the Church of Jesus Christ. For God loved this world, so that every person, every nation, all of life might know, feel and respond to the will and the purposes God has in mind.

Allow me to try to draw four word pictures of life, pictures which may depict for us our life, our thoughts, our response to the God we know through Jesus Christ.

1. *Rubber band.* The first picture is that of a rubber band. During one of the few breaks we had in a demanding workshop schedule someone presented us with this problem.

We were told to place a rubber band around the center of our hand and to take it off by the dexterity and flexibility of our fingers without the aid of the other hand, or rubbing it against anything.

It was a rather humorous sight to see about thirty persons going through all kinds of contortions trying to remove a rubber band. This is the first picture — A Rubber Band.

2. *Lifeless Body.* The second picture is a painful one to look at. It is a lifeless body of a fifteen year old boy lying on a sandy beach. This boy was attending summer camp. He went swimming alone and developed cramps and exhaustion in deep water beyond the reach of the life guard. This boy would not have been in camp if his church had not believed in him enough to pay most of his way. A boy who left home joyful, elated, and expectant, but who returned home silent–never to speak or to gladden the home again. That is the second picture — a lifeless boy on a sandy beach.

3. *Souvenir Counter.* In resort towns the demand for souvenirs is tremendous. This store met well the demands. The counter was 6 feet wide and over 50 feet long. It was filled with trinkets, pictures,

photographs, towels, scarves, anything you could think of or had ever seen — they had it. But this counter was not the ordinary run of the mill souvenirs. They were much too expensive for that. They were speciality items that appealed to and attracted the animal instincts of people.

You may well ask — What was I doing there? I too, was looking for souvenirs to take to my family. What attracted me were two women who were admiring these things that came straight from the Devil's Workshop. "Oh, isn't this cute?" one would say. "My husband would like this," the other would answer. Picture three — Souvenir Counter.

4. *Bowed Heads.* I hope I can draw with words a picture of "Bowed Heads" with such intensity and meaning that you and I will never forget it. It is a picture of young people with their heads and their hearts bowed in commitment to Jesus Christ and the church.

I have seen it happen with only logs for pews, a campfire for an altar, and the trees forming the walls and the roof of the sanctuary. I have seen it happen in services of commitment and dedication led by the young people themselves.

Despite all the criticism and judgments that are made against young people, when young persons are given the opportunity and provided the challenge under the proper kind of motivation they will dedicate their lives to the highest and best they know. They will sacrifice themselves for the future and they will trust God to lead them into that future.

At times I get fed up with us parents. When the

young people are challenged and they respond, the parents come along and try to talk them out of it. "It is all right for someone elses' kid to join the Peace Corps. It is all right for someone else to give their lives in service to Jesus Christ through the church, but not my kids–I have plans for them. You just stay close enough to the church to be good and stay out of trouble, but don't get so close that you will become committed," The fourth picture — Bowed Heads.

I have sketched briefly these four pictures. Let me try to fill in a few details and I encourage you to add your own in your own thinking and contemplation.

First, the rubber band. This represents to me so much of the futility of life. Energy is expended, time is used. Even if the rubber band is removed, what has been accomplished–Nothing. There are far too many rubber band snappers in our world and in the church with no sense of purpose or mission, no direction to their lives, no sense of obligation or responsibility for what they do.

Second, the lifeless body. There is tragedy and sadness in life. Some person in the blossom of life, some family in the midst of great hope and promise and "pow"—there is a tragedy–a death–an accident–an incurable illness and the dreams, the hopes, the desires, the ambitions crushed, ruined, broken.

There is a life-less body in nearly everyone's experience. It was for God, as His Son hung on the cross. Life is not just a matter of trying to escape tragedy, it is more of a matter of learning how we can respond to it and live through it. If there is one thing the crucifixion of Jesus Christ ought to tell us, it is the truth that there is a way through the tragedy of life. There is a way to get in touch with that Resurrection Power that will weave back together the broken strands in the tapestry of life. Not just to patch a hole, but to make it a beautiful and creative part of the picture.

We must hasten to the third picture — Souvenir Counter. This picture reveals the warped sense of values of our culture. People are leading such meaningless lives, the only thing they can find pleasure in, is the souvenir counters of life. Many of them are good people, they have nice homes, they have comfortable jobs, they have all the security this life can afford. They live and act out their lives without any sense of God being any part of it. These persons are the successful rubber band snappers in life. When they are hit with tragedy, their first question is: "Why did God let this happen to me?" This group will stand before the world and the great problems with which we are confronted and say everything is all right, and continue to play with the souvenirs.

The fourth picture — Young people bowing before God Almighty, the One who has created them, the One who seeks to redeem them, and now in grateful response to this great God, they are saying, "Here is my life — use it for Your purposes."

I have seen a beautiful Roman Catholic chapel on an Indian Reservation in northern Minnesota filled with young people kneeling–praying the rosary. The one bit of light in their entire life is that church.

I have seen young people make their commitment and dedicate their lives in a tabernacle in Kansas, with

69

a roof on poles and straw on dirt floor for carpeting and a plank between two posts for an altar.

We are witnessing commitment in many other fields: Sports heroes for example, thanking God for their athletic ability and using it as a means to influence others.

I read a short biography of Alan Shepherd, one of our first space men. He was a near genius. He was an authority in the area of astronautics, astrophysics, fuels, guidance systems, meterology, astronomy and geography. Asked why he volunteered for the space flights, he answered, "Because of the challenge of the worlds before us."

There is a world before us. It may not be pictured as graphically as the 25 ton, 28 feet diameter globe on the Babson Institute, but is before us and it is just as real. How do we picture ourselves before this world? Simply as Rubber Band Snappers, putting in our time? What shall our response be in a world filled with tragedy? Are we simply admiring and buying souvenirs and trinkets of life? Will we be among those who make that commitment of life that shall be a part of the plans and purposes of God? "Not everyone who says to me, 'Lord, Lord,' shall enter the kingdom of heaven but he who does the will of my Father." Matthew 7:21 And everyone who hears the words of Christ and does them shall be like that wise person who built his house on the rock and even when tragedy comes, "It did not fall because it had been founded on the Rock." Matthew 7:25

X.
A PARABLE OF BIRTHS
Genesis 1:27-28   John 3:1-15   John 11:17-27

Let me begin my sharing a series of vignettes or brief word pictures. At first they may seem to be unrelated but there is a thread of thought that runs through them and ties each of them together.

Just before our youngest child was about to be born, I was talking with the administrator of the small hospital where we lived. I asked if it would be possible to be present at the birth. She told me she did not know but would ask the doctor. As the time drew closer, I began to have second thoughts about asking for this special privilege. I did not mention it again to anyone. Soon the momentous day arrived and I took my wife to the hospital. While my wife was in the labor room, the doctor and I were having coffee together. As he got up to leave he said, "Would you like to watch the delivery?" I said, "You bet." "Come with me, you can scrub and get a gown."

Few experiences in my life so deepened my love and appreciation for my wife as did watching the delivery of our third son. A few impressions still linger with me. One was to see the rather dull blue body change to a rosy pink as the blood began to circulate about his body. Another was to discover what the doctor called the "world's finest hand cream" that covered his entire body. But to see the miracle of birth, first hand, was a tremendous experience.

Recently on television, Bill Moyers narrated a special telecast called "Born Again." It traced some of the present day religious movements. They interviewed Harold Hughes of Iowa and Martin Marty of Chicago. They talked to other persons who have had this "born again" experience. This is not something new, it was the way the church was founded. From the old camp meeting of yesteryear to the present day Billy Graham crusades, people are invited to share in this "born again" experience. To be "born again" is what the church is all about. Your experience of God may not be as dramatic as that of Chuck Colson. It may not be as cataclysmic as that of the Apostle Paul. You do not have to wear a "I Found It" button to prove your new birth. But that experience is the heart and core of the vitality and witness of the Church.

In the confirmation program I designed for my previous parishes, one of the requirements the young people were asked to do was to prepare a sermon and to deliver it publically. Corine gave her sermon on "Faith." I happened to be at her home a few days later. She told me, "Something happened to me. I have never felt God so real or so close to me as I did while giving my sermon." Today the spark plug behind the Christian Education program in one of our larger United Methodist Churches is Corine. She shared in the "born again" experience.

At a senior high camp in my group was a girl named Gladys. She came from a very undesirable home. One evening as we were talking together she said, "I would like to do something different with my life." Yes, she had found a way to be popular and acceptable especially to the boys. She knew it was not a love or an appreciation for her. She was being used and abused, and she knew it. We talked together about the directions her life could take. It was a long evening as we laughed and cried and prayed. But something happened to Gladys that night. I lost track of Gladys and forgot all about her. But one day a young lady came up, gave me a big hug and said, "I'm Gladys, remember me?" And then with tears coming to her eyes she said, "Thank you for helping me to be proud of myself. I'm married. These are my two children." Gladys had the "born again" experience.

What would take a boy who had been born and raised on a farm in North Dakota, who had every intention of continuing to farm with his father, who had no money, and set him on the road to the ministry? One day, I told my pastor, "I would like to be a minister." A peace came into my life, money came for the schooling, and I stand before you today to say the "born again" experience is a fact and a necessity of our life in Jesus Christ and His Church.

There are three kinds of birth experiences. The birth of a child into this world, the new birth of coming alive to God and finally the birth of our spirits into the home being prepared for us now.

Hallock was one of the most delightful older gentlemen I have ever known. He always had a smile on his face, and always ready with some quip or joke. Life had not been easy for him. He worked most of his life as a common laborer. His wife's lengthy illness had drained most of their savings. I was with Hallock the afternoon he had to decide whether or not to put his wife on a respirator which would have only prolonged certain death. That evening, as we sat together, Hallock holding one of his wife's hands and I holding the other, she died. Life was never the same for Hallock after that. The smile came only occasionally. The quips and jokes were not heard as often. He had not been feeling well, so he checked into the hospital. They found some minor ailments that could be corrected, but they really have no medicine for a broken heart. He was to be released from the hospital in a day or two, so I went up to see him that evening. We talked for a while and finally I said, "Let me read a verse or two of scripture and then we will have a prayer." He agreed. Before I had finished, his grip on my hand went limp. The "amen" to that prayer was not spoken to Hallock by me, it was spoken to Hallock directly to God.

There is a common thread through each of these changing experiences of life. They are the birth experiences of life. There is our natural birth. There is our spiritual birth. There is our birth into everlasting life. When we look at these three experiences, we find these common threads. First, we stand in the midst of a mystery we do not really understand, but it happens. Life itself is a mystery filled with questions.

Who can understand how a single egg can be fertilized and it grows and develops into a life? Who can understand what happens to a person's mind and heart so that they will make a radical change in what they are doing or the direction they are headed? Who can understand how a life that is headed down hill, or if at best at a low level, will be lured and enticed to walk the high road of life? Who can understand what happens when a person dies? The birth experiences of life are a mystery. But they are real. They are our experience.

A second common thread in these birth experiences of life is that we are aware that God is present in an unusual way. Anyone who has seen a new life emerge from its mother can sense and know the presence of God. There is joy, peace and elation when a person through new and deeper commitment discovers the reality of the presence of God in their lives. To be in a room where a death has just taken place, is to be in the "Holy of Holies" of God. The life of the person has left the physical house, but in that moment one becomes aware of the presence of God and the assurance that He is there to welcome that person into their new place of abiding. In the birth experiences of life, we are aware of God's presence in an unusual way.

A third common thread is that these birth experiences are transitions from one life to another. Our natural birth is the transition from a life dependent on the mother to an independent life. Our spiritual birth is the transition from our independent life to a life dependent upon and directed by God. Our death is the transition experience from this temporal life to

75

the everlasting life. The birth experiences of life are the transition experiences from one life to another.

There are three conclusions to be made from these birth experiences. There is a future before us after each birth experience and that future is one of unlimited possibility. Whenever we see a new baby, we "ooh" and "aah" and we wonder what will its future be? Who but God knows the tremendous possibility that lies within each new life? Who but God knows the seed for greatness that lies deep within each child? A greatness that will either be stunted or come to blossom and fruition by the way it is nurtured.

We come to our second birth experience when we come alive to God in new ways and life takes on a special meaning, a new direction, a new purpose for living. There is no one but God who can predict what will happen when even the most unlikely give their lives to God, to follow His direction, to fulfill His will. The world is waiting and searching for those persons who will experience this second birth so that God's will may be done on this earth, so our energies, powers and abilities will be guided and directed by God.

Humankind has never believed that death is the end. Death marks the beginning of a new future to be lived in that nearer presence of our Creator and our Maker. This is the first conclusion to be drawn, there is a tremendous, unlimited future that lies ahead, after each of our birth experiences.

The second conclusion is that God is ready to share and to guide us into that future. We are not left alone, to rely on our own resources. God is ready and willing and able to guide us into that future. We may not know the future, but our faith is in him who does. No parent knows the future of their children, but with a faith in God, they will do the best they can. No person who experiences the second birth says, "I can do it myself." But with faith and trust in God to lead, they will reach out toward the horizons of possibility for their future. Death is the ultimate test of our faith in God. It is now outside our realm of decision and action, but our faith tells us God is ready and willing to guide.

The third conclusion is that whatever the future, it is of God and it is good. This is our experience in our natural birth and our spiritual birth. It is of God and it is good. It is our faith that since death is within God's design for life, it is of God and we are confident it is good.

"In the image of God, He created him; male and female He created them and God blessed them and said, 'Be fruitful and multiply.'" Genesis 1:27 & 28 Our natural birth is of God. "Unless one is born of water and the Spirit, He cannot enter the kingdom of God." John 3:5 Our spiritual birth is of God. "I am the resurrection and the life; he who believes in me, though he die, yet shall he live." John 11:25 Our death is our birth into the nearer presence of God.

XI.

A PARABLE OF THE PHOENIX
Romans 12:2

There are over one hundred kinds of chameleon. Some have the ability to change their color to match their surroundings. Scientists tell us that changes in temperature, light or their own feelings control these changes in color.

We have the same ability to change our colors, only it is more highly developed. We turn blue when we are cold, a change in temperature. We get tanned with exposure to the sun, a change in light. Our faces get red when we are angry or embarrassed, a change in feelings.

A chameleon is known for its ability to adapt with color changes.

A dinosauer is a name given to a group of reptiles that lived on the earth millions of years ago. They ranged in size from 80 feet long to two and a half feet long, from 85 tons to 85 pounds. Some were flesh eaters, others were vegetarians. Some walked on all four feet, others walked upright on two feet. Some had extremely small brains and reproduced their young by laying eggs. The dinosauer no longer exists. Scientists estimate it may have taken from ten to twenty million years but the dinosauer is now extinct because it could not adapt to changing surroundings and circumstances.

The Phoenix is a bird of Greek mythology. It is a bird that has never lived but the story about it lives on. There was only one such bird. It would live 500 years, fly into an open fire and burn itself. Out of the ashes a new, young, dynamic and beautiful Phoenix bird emerged. What Greek mythology has done for us is to take a great spiritual truth and put it into a myth or story form. The Greeks used the Phoenix as a symbol, the dramatic idea of rebirth and immortality.

In our text, Paul is writing to a small, persecuted group of Christians in Rome. The pressure is on and the odds against their survival are slim. Paul knew this and thus he proclaimed if the church was to survive and grow, they could not "be conformed to this world."

The pressure on us to conform is just as powerful as it was on those Christians in Rome, only it is more subtle. We are pressured from every side to fit in — don't rock the boat — make things go smoothly. In our area there are several Hutterite Colonies. When they come to town the locals laugh and snicker at their dress. We smile because they all dress alike. But look at the way we dress. Some new style comes along, whether it be the length of skirt or type of eye glasses, and the stampede is on to be in style — to conform.

Politicians in their desire to be elected spend huge sums taking public opinion polls and then announce, "That's where I stand."

We are amused with chameleons taking on the color and pattern of their environment, but there is nothing amusing about chameleon Christians, those who are just a reflection of the world about us. God's word commands us not to be chameleon Christians. Taking on the color and the pattern of life around us is not God's way. We are to transform life about us by demonstrating in our own lives what is God's will.

If a chameleon is not the model for our life in Christ, neither is the dinosauer. No one followed the words of our text better than the dinosauer, "do not be conformed." The world about him was changing but the dinosauer absolutely refused to change or adapt and no one is more dead and gone than the dinosauer. No dinosauer Christian either is God's word to us.

There are few groups of people who cause the leaders of the church more ulcers and heart aches than the dinosauer Christian. For them, there is no greater sin than to have something changed. If being a chameleon, adapting to and accepting all changes and taking on the color of our surroundings is not the way; if being a dinosauer, resisting all the changes of the world is not the way, what then is the way?

The way is illustrated by the Phoenix. The Phoenix is our symbol. For in Jesus Christ we are in touch with a transforming power. In Jesus Christ, we have access to the source of renewal for life and spirit. Out of the dead ashes of what was, we shall rise to accept and to be what God has in mind.

The greatest achievements in life, in history, in the church have not come from those who simply reflected what is. No great achievements have ever come from those who were firmly cemented in the past. Think of Lincoln, or Churchill, or Kennedy. They had a vision and the insight that transformed them. They were able to point their nation into new directions. Take the prophets and the Apostles. Persons like John Wesley or Martin Luther, or persons like Kagawa or Albert Schweitzer or Martin Luther King, who refused to accept public opinion polls for their directive, refused to be enslaved to the comfortable ideas of yesterday. They had a vision of something new.

The symbol of the Christian is not the chameleon or the dinosauer but the Phoenix. To die in order to rise with the resurrection power of Jesus Christ is a central truth of the Gospel. The key word is not to conform or to be a conformist, but to transform, "Be transformed by the renewal of your minds."

We are afraid, afraid to die, afraid to put to death our old ideas, our worn out ways; afraid of what God might ask us to be or to do. So we cling to our past, afraid to give up the comfortable and easy ways we have made.

The call of Jesus Christ in our text is neither a sell-out to what everyone else is doing or a clinging to the ways of yesterday. Rather it is a call to new vitality, by being transformed. The voice we need to hear is the voice of Jesus Christ above the noise and clatter about us. The voice that says, "I am the way, the truth and the life." John 14:6 The church is not to make the fashion of the day and the church is not to be shackled by what was. The church is to demonstrate the transforming power of Jesus Christ. Our purpose is to bring men and women, boys and girls into touch with this transforming power of Jesus Christ so that God's will and God's purpose can be done.

Not the chameleon, not the dinosauer, but the Phoenix is our symbol. We believe life can be transformed. We may have tried to hide from it like a chameleon. We may have tried to keep things as they were like a dinosauer. But in every generation and in every church there are those who know and give witness to this transforming power of Jesus Christ. But what is important is to affirm it can happen today and it can happen to us. Let the Phoenix be the symbol of transforming our lives and the life about us.

No chameleon kind of faith in Christ, no dinosauer kind of faith in Christ, not conformed, but transformed, not adapted but remade. Like the Phoenix rising from the ashes of our past to be transformed by the renewal of our minds, that we constantly prove what is the will and purpose of God for our lives, for our church and our world. Then we will know and experience what is good and acceptable and perfect.

XII.
A PARABLE OF THE POTTER
Jeremiah 18:1-6

Come with me on a short journey. We will leave the well beaten roads which we usually follow and take a little foot path. We will follow a narrow, winding path that runs over the hill and through the valley to the potter's house. We will stop at the potter's house to hear a word or two from God.

As we follow this narrow winding path to the potter's house, we will not go alone. We are able to see more if we take someone with us who has eyes that have been trained to see through long and rich experience.

The one we will be going with is the great prophet Jeremiah. We are all the more anxious to go with him because God has just told him to arise and go down to the potter's house.

We soon notice something is radically wrong with our guide. Jeremiah is not himself. A psychiatrist would say Jeremiah is in a deep depression. We would say Jeremiah has a case of the blues. Jeremiah is ready to lay down his God given tasks, throw up his hands and quit. Why look, Jeremiah is crying! Now Jeremiah is no weakling, no baby, he is one of the great prophets of God, but he has come to the end of his rope. People sneer at him — spit at him. He is accused of being unpatriotic. Others are seeking his life. Jeremiah sees the direction his beloved nation is heading and he knows that unless there is a change they are headed for destruction.

He is saying to himself, "I preach and no one changes, I call but no one answers, I share a vision and no one responds, I plead and no one pays any attention, I warn and no one listens." "It is useless and I might as well give up and quit," Jeremiah is crying. Not for his own sins—anyone can cry over their own sins, but it takes a giant of a person to feel so deeply the sins of others that they will weep for them.

We find Jeremiah discouraged, despondent and depressed.

God needs Jeremiah. God needs Jeremiah now, but he cannot use him in this state of mind and soul. Talking to Jeremiah won't help because he cannot hear. You have heard the old saying, "In one ear and out the other," but we never hear "In one eye and out the other." If God is to use Jeremiah, and if Jeremiah is to be the person God needs, God must illustrate, must act out the message. God is saying, "Jeremiah, you cannot hear what I have to say but maybe you can see and have demonstrated what you need to understand."

We arrive at the potter's house. Let's go in with Jeremiah and look over the potter's shoulder and watch him as he works. Maybe we too can hear a word or two from God.

The first thing that strikes us is the simplicity of his house. Everything there is simple. But many great things are simple. Most great people have been really quite simple. Think of some great words—light, life, truth, faith, hope, love, home, peace, God. They are all simple words. All we see in the potter's house are simple things like the material, the machinery, the potter, and the helper.

1. *The material — Clay.* Over in the corner is the pile of clay. It probably doesn't cost him a thing to get it except a little labor. Dirt — clay. The stuff our kids drag and track into the house on rainy days. The stuff that gets on our clothes and we send them to the cleaners. The stuff that fills the air and covers everything on dry, windy days.

Useless, no good clay when properly processed and brought to the potter becomes utensils and vessels of usefulness or works of art.

"Then the Lord God formed man of the dust from the ground." Genesis 2:7a We are clay shaped into persons by God. But that's not all we are. "And God breathed into his nostrils the breath of life, and man became a living being." Genesis 2:7b

Here is the word of God from the potter:

If properly processed and given into the hands of Jesus Christ, the great potter, we can be fashioned into vessels and utensils of beauty and usefulness. The potter's skillful touch and sure hand can prepare us for service in God's kingdom.

We have had a parade of persons through our church office seeking assistance. Then the word of the Lord came to me, "Don't you see? Can't you understand — every last one of us was created from the dust of the earth." I can never call any person the scum of earth. I will pray, work and seek to bring every person to the master potter. Seek to place them in his hands and watch them grow and develop into a vessel of usefulness and beauty.

And what about you and me. Have we allowed Jesus Christ to fashion and shape our lives? Are we only pretty ornaments on the shelf of life or are we on the daily table of the Lord being used by Him to give food and drink to those about us?

2. *The Machinery.* Our eyes shift now from the potter to the instruments he uses — a potter's wheel and a piece of string.

The wheel is a horizontal disk, 10-12 inches across, mounted on a small plain table. The wheel is powered by a large heavy kick wheel which the potter keeps going around and around—now fast, now slow, all determined by how fast the potter wants it to go. It has a dull, wearisome sound as it goes in monotonous revolutions.

I said to myself, "If all I had to work with was that wheel, day in and day out, month in and month out, year after year, I would get absolutely bored. If only once in awhile it would go up or down, or backwards or sideways just anything to change. Yet it was on that wheel with all its monotonous rounds that the potter shaped his beautiful vessels. Then the word of the Lord came to me, "Don't you see? Can't you understand as you watch the potter?" It is in these ordinary circumstances, the common experiences of everyday life, the monotonous things we do day after day where most of life is lived. We get up in the morning, eat breakfast, do the dishes, get dressed, off to work, off to school, lunch, dinner, do the dishes, do a few things, then to bed and then another day. Most of the things we do, we do every day.

On occasions some great things do happen. But for most of us, it is the same daily grind. Yet, it is in the midst of the monotonous, daily routine that the great potter seeks to shape our lives. We are seldom, if ever, shaped by the great events of life. How we act or react in the great events can be predicted by our shaping in the day to day experiences. God is saying, just as no life is unimportant, so no day is unimportant. Each day is a day to be shaped and molded by Jesus Christ.

Now I said he had two simple tools—the wheel and the string. Now watch how he takes that string, draws it tight and slips it under the vessel and cuts it free from the wheel for working and finishing. All that really happened on the wheel was to give shape to the vessel. The string was used to cut it free from its monotonous existence so that it might be used. The word of the Lord came to me. "Don't you see, can't you understand?" We need to be cut free from our daily monotonous existence to be of service. Are we so deeply and firmly set upon the wheel of life so that all we do is to go round and round in circles and never get anywhere? To be of service and usefulness, we need to be set free by the master potter.

Oh, how we resist being set free. But we will never be of service until the master potter who seeks to shape and mold us sets us free for service.

3. *The Potter.* Now, we are ready to look at the potter himself, He is no novice — he is an old hand at this shaping business. He is wise. He pays strict

attention to his work, carefully shaping and molding each piece. Just when I thought he was done, he would add a touch here, a little shaping there until he was satisfied with what he was doing. For a moment, I took my eyes off the potter and looked around the room for the patterns he was using. He has no pictures or models on the wall, no books or illustrations. Why, he never even asked us for suggestions of what to make next. Maybe he would make a cup or a saucer, a plate or a bowl, a vase or a pitcher. And as we look at each piece the potter created, we notice that no two are exactly alike, there are no duplicates and there do not seem to be any extras.

Then, the word of the Lord came to me: "Don't you see, don't you understand?" The master potter has a plan for everything he creates. We may not see that plan, we may not know the plan, but is it so important that I know the plan or is it more important to trust and believe in the plan of the potter?

Jesus Christ, the Great Potter is shaping and molding each piece in the daily experiences of life. Jesus Christ, the Great Potter, is creating and forming each piece with its own individual uniqueness so that there are no duplicates, no extras. Why don't we slip our life into his hands, to be shaped and molded? Let us rejoice and celebrate the reality that each of us is unique and different, each of us have our place and purpose, each of us have our place in God's master plan.

4. *The Helper.* Standing almost unnoticed in the corner was the potter's helper. There he was working unnoticed and overlooked. We are almost ready to say, "What are you doing here?" He spoils the whole

scene. He takes a shovel of clay, adds some water and begins to mix, knead and trowel the clay. As the potter was removing the vase from the wheel, he would have the next batch of clay ready for the potter. Occasionally, he would sweep up left over wads and bits of clay and put it back into the vat to be reworked. His job looked like the kind of job anyone of us could do. And then the word of the Lord came to me, "Don't you see, don't you understand?" Your task in life is to be the helper of that Great Potter. It is not your job or responsibility to shape and mold the vessels to your plan or ideas, that is the responsibility of the Great Potter. You are simply to bring the clay to the Potter. Anybody can do that. Anyone can do that if they know where the clay is and where the Potter is.

God is seeking to pick up the broken, scattered piece of my life and yours, to rework them, to place them again on the wheel for shaping into something beautiful. He wants to refashion our lives into vessels of usefulness.

We have seen all we can see in the potter's house, but did we see and understand what God wanted us to see and understand?

The value of each person,

The importance of each day,

The power and ability of Jesus Christ to shape life,

My task and responsibility to bring persons to Jesus Christ,

This is God's message to us from our journey to the potter's house.

XIII.
A PARABLE OF THE CEDARS
Matthew 7:24-28

We had an absolutely delightful vacation in Glacier Park. The majestic snow covered mountains and glaciers, the crystal clear waters of the lakes and streams, the beauty and color of the wild flowers, the peaceful green of the trees, the unique style of the lodges, the hikes along narrow paths through the forests, the company of family and good friends, combined to make a vacation that was most enjoyable and created a deep desire to return.

The Trail of the Cedars is a narrow foot path in a secluded and protected valley where huge cedar trees grow. Some of these cedars were so large it would take four to six of us holding hands to reach around the trunk. They stood 100 to 150 feet tall. The path was like walking on a carpeted floor with a thick bed of fallen needles and pine cones. It was a spongy cushion over a foot deep.

Slowly we ambled along the trail, gazing at the magnificent beauty of this valley. The many different shades and colors of green, the water dripping down over the rock formations causing thick moss and ferns to grow; the babbling singing waters of the nearby stream, and the size and number of the beautiful cedars, all this and much more in one little beautiful valley.

The path led up along the mountain side to Avalanche Lake. As we went upward, the trail became more difficult. It was hard, rocky and narrow. The mountain sides do not have the abundant growth of the valley. We paused to rest about 1,000 feet above the valley and discovered that the cedars continued to grow, high along the mountain side.

The cedars on the mountain sides are tall and slim, and not nearly so abundant. We discover later that the cedars are all about the same age, but up here they are only one-tenth to one-fourth the size.

On the mountainside, most of the trees are standing erect, but down in the valley, many of the cedars have fallen over. The cedars in the valley have shallow root systems. They have ample food and water near the surface. When an occasional strong wind blows through the valley, many of them will topple over.

The cedars on the mountain sides have sunk their roots solidly and deeply into the rock crevices as they search to find nourishment.

To the casual observer, wood from cedar trees would have the same use. But that is not true. The trees are carefully selected and harvested for a particular purpose. If strong wood is needed, wood that can bear heavy loads, wood that can bend without breaking., the cedars from the mountain sides are selected. When wood is used for decorative purposes, like paneling, or trim around windows and doors, the cedars in the valley are harvested.

The Parable of the Cedars prompts three questions: 1) Can we stand the wind? 2) Where are our roots? 3) How shall we be used?

First can we stand the winds? Because of the very nature of the mountains and the weather systems, this area is subjected to constant and often violent winds. As the weather systems move from the west to the east, the winds are pushed upward on the western slopes, and passing over the mountain peaks, slip down the eastern slopes like a huge playground slide. Winds have been clocked as high as 120 miles per hour. There is no such thing as a day without wind on the mountain sides.

Protected on three sides by mountain ridges, the Valley of the Cedars seldom has any wind. But if by some quirk of nature the winds shift and they are channeled back into this valley, and if they reach much over 50 miles per hour, these huge trees go tumbling down like bowling pins.

Can we stand the winds of life? Some people are caught in the storms of life, and others seldom seem to have a windy day. But all of us, at one time or another will find ourselves in the middle of a storm. Tragedy, sorrow, illness, fear, worry, grief, sin are realities of life. The winds will blow, sometimes violently. They did for Jesus Christ, for Paul, for John Wesley, for Martin Luther King and they will for you and for me. Can we stand the wind?

The answer to the question, can we stand the wind is answered by the next question prompted by this parable—where are our roots? There is only one way to test where our roots are and that is to let the winds blow. Unless the winds do blow, we will not sink our roots very deeply. As long as we are well fed and watered, as long as we are well cared for, as long as we have what we think we want and need, we are not very likely to sink our roots very deeply.

We have no reason to fear the winds, if we have sunk our roots deeply and securely into the sustaining, life-giving power, strength and love of God through Jesus Christ.

A commentator on the Church in America said that he feared for the church in America because we have lost our ability to suffer. I take that to mean he believes our roots are so shallow that if the strong winds blow, we will not be able to stand.

The opportunities are before us to pray, to worship, to serve, to study, to learn, to share in the word and to live in the spirit of Jesus Christ. Each of us must seek to sink our roots into that which will hold us safely and securely when the winds blow. Where are our roots?

How shall we be used? If I ever have the opportunity to design and build a home, at least one room will be paneled with cedar. The grain patterns are wild and varied. They are so different and most beautiful when finished. They provide an unparalleled beauty. But for the beams in the floor and the rafters in the roof, I want something that is strong and durable, something that is able to withstand the weight. I want trees that have grown high on the mountain side.

We could describe the membership of the church by this parable. Some are just beautiful wall paneling, good to look at, nice to have around, but we could almost get along without them. Besides we have to be careful, they are so easily scratched and it takes so much time trying to polish the scratches and marks.

Others could be described like the beams in the floor

and roof. One doesn't know they are around but they are there, supporting, holding it together. They can be tromped on, jumped on and kicked, but they will stay in place and do the job.

We could go through this fruitless task of dividing people into paneling and floor beams, but the real question is, how shall I be used? Am I one of those who support, who guide, who strengthen? Shall I be one of those who can be counted upon, to hold things together?

If life can be compared to this Parable of the Cedars, how shall I be used? Only you can provide that answer.

Long before Jimmy Carter brought national attention to Plains, Georgia, Americus Georgia was made famous by the courageous and saintly Clarence Jordan. Clarence Jordan was a farmer who had an earned doctor's degree in New Testament Greek. Jordan believed it was more important to try to live the Word than to teach it, so he sought to develop a community that would literally put into practice the words of Jesus Christ.

Clarence Jordan translated the New Testament from the Greek into everyday English. His translation is one that I use often. I will close this morning by reading our text from Clarence Jordan's "Cotton Patch Version of the New Testament," with a few Blumer additions.

> The person who hears these words of mine and acts on them, shall be like the wise person who built his house on the rock (with cedar high off the mountainside). Down came the rain, up

rose the flood, out lashed the winds, they all cut at that house but it didn't fall. It was on a rock foundation (with strong, tough cedars).

The person who hears these words of mine, and fails to act on them shall be like an idiot who built his house on the sand (with cedar paneling from the valley). The rain came down, the floods rose up, the winds lashed out. They all cut at that house and it fell! And my what a collapse.

XIV.
A PARABLE OF THE GARDENER
Mark 4:1-20

I will share a modern day parable, "Change," by Alice Rollins.

"One day as I chanced to wander into a blacksmith shop, I watched the blacksmith at work as he put the iron into the fire. I saw how he added more fuel to make the fire and used the bellows to make the heat more intense. I saw him take the molten ore and shape it, and then beat it into the shape he had need of. Whether it be a spear or a sword, a ploughshare or a pruning hook, it had become a tool to be used. I wondered. The blacksmith had changed the ore with fire and hammer into a tool; it was rigid and it would stay that way for many a year until heat or force would change.

"Again another day, I chanced to watch a potter at work with the clay. It was soft and so easy to handle. I watched as he rolled it and squeezed it until it took the shape he had planned. He colored it and glazed it, then he put it in the kiln to harden it with long slow heat. Whether it became a cup with which to receive or a pitcher from which to give, it had become a thing of beauty. Again I wondered. The potter had changed the clay to a thing of beauty and it was so brittle. It would stay that way until someone dashed it to the ground.

"Yet another time I wandered into a garden to watch a gardener at work among his flowers. He too used the soil, he planted the seeds in it. He used the slow, natural heat of the sun. He knew the seeds held within them the secret of what they would become. The gardener gave care—water when the rains did not come; food when the soil was starved. He protected them from the aphids that would sap their strength. At times, he could clip a small growth that would bring strength from a single, lovely flower. But the plants continued to grow and change. As they grew they never failed to give in beauty or joy. The gardener had a real part in the growth that came. He did not beat or fan the flame to make a hard set tool. He did not mold the shape he desired into a thing of beauty. He had guided the growth.

"I wondered. How does real change come? Has heat and force made me a rigid tool? Have I become a brittle thing, or am I changing, growing, giving?

"May I too learn the lesson they teach–
The blacksmith, the potter, the gardener, each
As he performs his task and does it well.
But from each of these, I know I can tell,
And come to know what changes are the kind
That make a difference in man's mind.

Dear God, help me learn from all I see
To grow and change–never, ever to be
So rigid, so brittle, so firmly set–
That new ideas, the people I have met
Cannot help me learn and grow to be
One who is growing more and more like thee."

–From Child Guidance, October 1962

> With many such parables he spoke the word to
> them, as they were able to hear it; he did not
> speak to them without a parable, but privately
> to his own disciples, he explained everything.
> Mark 4:33-34

The blacksmith, the potter, the gardener are three
approaches to life. To me Jesus Christ was not a
blacksmith or a potter, but he was the Master
Gardener of Life. He did not beat or force his ideas
and his concerns with hammer and fire. He sought to
guide the growth of the seeds of greatness that God
places into every life. He sought to open the doorways
and the pathways to God, and guide persons to grow
in that experience.

Jesus must have thought of himself as a Master
Gardener, because of his constant use of natural and
growing things to illustrate his messages. He spoke of
the seed and the soils, the lilies of the field, the
mustard seed, tares among the wheat, the growing
crops, and harvest time. He saw his mission from God
to guide and to care for the seeds of God that are
planted in this world, and in your life and mine.

1. *This parable can be set against different situations. Think of it in terms of government.*

The blacksmith is the dictatorship form of government. The will of the leader is forged through his
power. Now we know not all dictatorships are evil,
some are good and even necessary, but many of them
are cruel, unjust and corrupt.

There are very few monarchies left in our world—
the king and queen form of government. Where they
do exist, it is much like a beautiful piece of pottery set

upon the mantle of life. With all the pomp, majesty and royalty, they are more ornamental than useful.

A democracy can be described as the gardener. The strength and the vitality of the government is in the people. The leader's role is to guide and direct the concerns and needs of the people. The power is not in one person or one family, the power is with the people.

2. *This parable can be used with the family.* My grandfather was one of the most saintly persons I ever knew. But my father told me he could never remember ever setting foot into grandfather's bedroom. His bedroom was off limits. He ruled his six sons and two daughters with an iron hand. His word was law. His decisions were never questioned to his face.

Our families are not steel to be forged with heat and fire and pounding.

I like to see persons dressed up in bright, pretty clothes. I admire the way some women can use make up. But clothes and make up can become only so much paint to cover up the warts and pimples on a person's soul, instead of enhancing and highlighting one's inner beauty.

If our lives and our families become things of fragile beauty, we are in for some rude awakenings. As we move along life's pathway, with its bumps and pitfalls, our families will be broken and dashed to the ground.

How much better it is to see our families as individual persons who have within them vital seeds of life that need to be nurtured and cared for so that the unique flower or fruit God had in mind, can come to fruition.

Not hammering it into what I want, or making it

look beautiful, when the real beauty is gone, but to guide the growth and allow God's beauty to come to reality.

3. *This parable can be applied to education.* In the so-called "good old days" of the McGuffy readers, a limited amount of knowledge was taught to the tune of the hickory stick. That is the blacksmith approach with the education being beat into a person.

Then we went through a stage called "Progressive Education," where each was to do their own thing. But we didn't really know what that "own thing" was. It sounded good, looked pretty, but like the potter, it did not accomplish the task.

We are seeing some tremendous things occurring in education. Each child is seen as someone unique, with unique talents, gifts and potential. The task of education is to find that uniqueness, to nurture it, to guide its growth. Thus we have children in elementary school doing college science and math. Or we have those who once were considered unable to learn, now caring for themselves, gainfully employed at simple tasks. There are more persons learning at every age-level, and at every level of comprehension than ever before. For like the gardener, the educator is seeking to nurture the seed of what a person can become. Not to beat it in, not to make the child what we want, but to nurture the seed so they can become what God intends.

4. *This parable can be applied to the church.* There was a day in the early Protestant church and in the Roman Catholic church, where the blacksmith method was the way to operate. I can recall some of the old revival preachers, who with fire

and pounding, or by giving church edicts, shared the faith.

There are churches today who emphasize the beauty of their building, the greatness of the liturgy, or their past accomplishments. It is just so much ornamental pottery.

The effective church today is where there is responsible participation. The emphasis is upon the growth and nurture of persons in the faith. There change is evident. There is new response and application of faith to personal needs. There is a challenge to match the call of Christ to present situations. New avenues and doorways are being opened to follow the leading of Jesus Christ.

5. *The parable can be applied to you and me.* At times, I feel there are those who want to take out the hammer and the anvil and try to beat a greater response out of persons by making such statements as: "If they won't give, if they won't respond, kick them out."

Others will talk about how careful we have to be so we won't hurt anyone's feelings. "We had better treat them with kid gloves or they will leave." Seeing people as fragile pieces of pottery, or persons who need to be hammered into shape is not the way of Christ.

I fear we know neither the life our Lord and Savior lived, nor the words he taught, nor the fellowship of persons, he demonstrated. Yet there are times when we like to pound people over the head or pour fire and brimstone upon them for not believing or acting in ways we expect.

Yes, we would like to spend our time and our energies

making the church look nice and pretty, or recall the way things used to be, like the potter. But who stands ready and willing to be a gardener? Who will nurture and guide the lives of others by sharing, by living, growing and by hearing Christ's kind of fruit?

If this parable illustrates approaches to life and faith, can we see ourselves in it?

Are we a blacksmith that wants to beat and pound? Are we potters who want to sit around like ornamental pieces? Or shall we hear Christ's call to cultivate and nurture the life and opportunities that He places before us, so that God's kingdom might come, and God's will be done right here on earth, where we live.

XV.
A PARABLE OF A BLOSSOM
Matthew 13:1-9; 18-23

In a workshop I attended recently we were divided into groups of five persons and asked to do the following: In one sentence describe an "Ideal Religious Community," pick a name for the community and draw a symbol of that community. We were given three hours to do it, and then return to the large group to share our work.

One of the groups had spent most of their time designing a symbol. It was strikingly beautiful and on several parts of the symbol they had written in words to describe what it meant to them. As they were sharing, I objected to those words. "A symbol is a symbol, let it speak as it is." I objected to their telling me what I thought it should mean to me. The lady who designed it became a bit miffed and told me what she thought of my criticism of her symbol. I was involved in a heated argument. Eventually we came to understand what each was saying and we both agreed that each of us was right. Then a few weeks later she sent me a poster, "Bloom Where You are Planted." I want to draw a few inferences from that poster, "Bloom Where You Are Planted."

1. Instead of blooming where we are planted, some of us want to be *transplanted*. We don't like where we

are, we don't like what we are doing, we don't want to be with those we are associated with and so we begin to dream. "If only I were someplace else. If only I were doing something else. If only I were somewhere else, then I could bloom and blossom."

It is my observation that those who are always in dreamland and hoping and praying to be transplanted into more favorable places, never make it. The ideal place, where conditions and events will match their hopes and dreams never comes. Such persons are always wanting to be transplanted instead of seeking to Bloom Where They Are Planted.

2. Instead of blooming where they are planted, some of us just *exist* where we are planted. There may be stalks and leaves, all the indications of fruitfulness but never any blossoms or fruit. There is promise of blossoms and fruit but as yet nothing—only existing. These who just exist where they are planted can be thought of as parasites. They receive and draw from the resources about them. They take and use that which others provide but never produce any blossoms or fruit. They just exist where they are planted.

3. Some *wilt* where they are planted. Again all the indications and possibilities for fruitfulness are there. The soil may be good and fertile. There is sunshine and rain. But they wilt because no roots were developed to take in the food, the water and the sunshine which is necessary for growth.

Life is a burden, and with its problems, it becomes just too much for them and they wilt there they are planted.

4. *But there are those who bloom where they are planted.* I have a picture of a pine tree that I took while hiking in the Rocky Mountains. It is the only tree on this mountain top. It has branches only on one side because the strong, prevailing winds which blow constantly kept blowing off the branches as they grew on the other side. But here was a tree that bloomed where it was planted. If that tree had a mind to think, I wonder how often it must have wished to be transplanted. It could have wilted, but no, it stood strong and tall, a bit misshapen but blooming where it was planted.

How can I, how can you, bloom where you are planted? To sincerely believe that where I am today is where God wants me to bloom. God expects me to blossom. God knows and God promises I can bloom where I am planted right now—today!

We can spend all of our time and energy wishing to be transplanted. We can exist like a parasite where we are planted, we can dry up, wilt, and die. Simply because we are not willing to believe we can bloom where we are planted, we deny the fact that God wants and expects us to blossom where we are today.

The means and grace are available to bloom and blossom where we are today. There are persons in this world, all around us, who want and need our love. There are persons in this world, all around us, who want and who need to love us. The sunshine and rain of life is persons. We will never bloom where we are planted unless we receive and we give love to persons.

The resources for growth are here—worship, prayer, service. This is the soil into which we need to sink our roots and receive into our souls and minds, the nutrients of the spirit.

Our faith and life cannot grow and develop in isolation from other persons. Our lives and witness cannot bloom and blossom without the resources of God through prayer and worship and service. Jesus illustrated it in our scripture reading of the seeds and the sower. It was not the sower who needed to change. The sower gave freely to all who would receive. The sunshine and the rain came in like amounts to all the places the seeds were sown. The seeds would grow and blossom into fruitfulness if — IF — if the conditions of the soil were right. It was not the sower, or the sunshine, or the seed that made the difference, the difference was in the soil. It is our ability to receive, our willingness to provide the conditions, our desire to grow and to bloom and to blossom that makes the difference. We are the soil into which the Word of God is sown by Jesus Christ. "And some fell on the paths." They wanted to be transplanted. "Some fell on rocky ground," they wilted. "Some fell among the thorns," they just existed. "Some fell on good soil," they bloomed where they were planted bringing forth thirty and sixty and a hundred fold.

XVI.
A PARABLE OF THE BUTTERFLY
John 12:24

One of the marvels of God's creation is the butterfly.

One year at a summer youth camp my partner was a lady who taught biology. We were taking a hike, and every time we came to a milkweed plant she would stop and carefully look the plant over. We would ask her what she was looking for and her answer was, "You will see." Finally she found what she was looking for. It was a green caterpillar worm. Carefully she placed the worm in a pouch she was carrying and added a few milkweed leaves.

Upon arriving back at camp she found a large glass jar. In the jar she placed a few stones, a little water, a short twig from a tree, a few milkweed leaves and the green caterpillar.

The jar became the center of attention. Everyone would stop to see what was happening. Everyone was picking milkweed leaves, far more than our green friend could ever consume.

One morning to the amazement of us all, the caterpillar was not there, but hanging from the twig was the most beautiful, delicate green cocoon with gold flecks. During the night the caterpillar had woven for itself this beautiful cocoon.

Camp came to an end and I asked if I could take the jar home. Again the jar became the center of attention for our young family and their neighborhood friends. We watched the cacoon change its color from its once beautiful green to a dark ugly brown. We too were in for a surprize. One morning the dark brown cocoon was shattered and sitting on a twig was a beautiful Monarch butterfly.

A tremendous transformation had taken place before our very eyes. From a green worm, to a cocoon, to a beautiful butterfly. The butterfly should be the symbol of our faith. Our faith in Jesus Christ is a faith which brings changes, drastic changes to our lives.

Jesus said "Unless a grain of wheat falls into the earth and dies, it remains alone, but if it dies, it bears much fruit." John 12:24 Our lives need to be changed! Our lives can be changed! It is a miracle to change a worm into a butterfly. But it is a greater miracle to have our lives changed so much that it is like being born again. But that is the hope and the possibility we have in God through Jesus Christ.

The butterfly is a symbol of the resurrection that can take place from this life to life eternal. Within all of us there is a desire to know what the life to come is like. I believe Jesus would say look around you, if a worm can change into a butterfly, will your transformation from this life to life eternal be anything less? "I am the resurrection and the life, he who believes in me, though he die, yet shall he live, and whoever lives and believes in me shall never die." John 11:24-25

As we reflect on this parable we find ourselves thinking too much of ourselves as ugly worms instead of beautiful butterflies. We need to see ourselves as persons whom God has created, persons with tremendous potential. God has placed within us a butterfly that is waiting to be released, a potential for beauty, a potential for life. But we have never allowed God to set us free.

We either are worms that move along seeking to fill our appetites, or we are all wrapped up in our cocoons.

Can we see ourselves, can we see our church as butterflies to have the beauty and possibility of what God has in mind to set us free for His glory and the work of His Kingdom?

Can we see those we love, who have gone to live in our Father's House with its many rooms, as those who like the butterfly have been released from their cocoons of sin and sorrow and suffering, to that person living in the nearer presence of God?

Oh, let the parable of the butterfly speak to our need.